Pith Instructions from my Teachers

Pith Instructions from my Teachers
James Gritz

Published by
The Sumeru Press Inc.
PO Box 75, Manotick Main Post Office,
Manotick, ON, Canada K4M 1A2

Text Copyright © 2023 by James Gritz
All photos by James Gritz except where noted

Editing by Kimberly Beek
Design by John Negru

ISBN 978-1-998248-00-1

All rights reserved. No part of this book may be reproduced, stored in a retrieval system, or transcribed in any form or by any means—electronic, mechanical, photocopying, recording, or otherwise—without the prior written permission of the publisher.

Library and Archives Canada Cataloguing in Publication

Title: Pith instructions from my teachers / James Gritz.
Names: Gritz, James, author.
Description: Includes bibliographical references.
Identifiers: Canadiana 20230564399 | ISBN 9781998248001
   (softcover)
Subjects: LCSH: Dharma (Buddhism) | LCSH: Buddhism—
   China—Tibet Autonomous Region.
Classification: LCC BQ7775 .G75 2023 | DDC 294.3/444—dc23

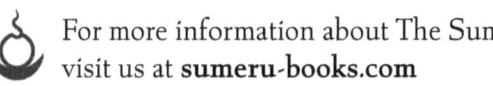

For more information about The Sumeru Press
visit us at **sumeru-books.com**

Contents

Foreword. 5
Preface 9
Introduction. 13

Chögyam Trungpa Rinpoche 17
Guadalupe Gonzales Rios. 43
Jigme Khyentse Rinpoche 61
Tsoknyi Rinpoche 75
Dzogchen Ponlop Rinpoche. 113
Dzongsar Khyentse Rinpoche. . . . 135
The 16th and 17th Karmapas 157
Mingyur Rinpoche 179

Conclusion 191
Suggested Reading 197
Glossary of Buddhist Terms. 199
Bibliography. 205

Foreword

I have known James for a number of years and admire his commitment to his spiritual path. Throughout the years he has made the effort to meet many great teachers of the past and present. Having the opportunity to meet with authentic teachers and receive their personal instructions is an extraordinary and precious thing in this world. I am happy that James has felt motivated to gather the instructions he has received from his teachers in this book. I hope it will not only inspire readers to seek out an authentic teacher and enter the guru-student relationship but will also help them to progress along the path towards freedom.

Jigme Khyentse Rinpoche
June 11, 2023

I dedicate this book to all my teachers,
holders of the precious practice lineages of Tibetan Buddhism.
May they continue passing on the profound pith instructions
of the Buddha until all beings are free.

James Gritz

Pith Instructions from my Teachers

If I am teaching you how to ride a bike, which actually is ironic, and I am your personal teacher, and as your personal teacher I am looking at you seeing there are certain personal weaknesses and strengths that you have that I know about, I have to tell you certain things that I may never tell anyone else. For example, let's say every time you are about to ride a bike I tell you to have a shot of tequila, because for you that is a necessity. This is what we call *man-ngag upadesha*, pith instructions. It is so important that this pith instruction has to help something, which is, of course, in this case, the ability for you to ultimately ride the bike.

Dzongsar Khyentse Rinpoche
– from Madhyamika Teachings in Vancouver, 1995

Preface

This book began after going through many of my old notebooks from seminars, teachings and retreats led by Buddhist teachers. I have been fortunate in this life. Not with business or wealth, which I have never been able to hold onto. But I've had the good fortune to travel the world as a photographer and experience amazing landscapes, people, and exotic cultures. However, the true reason my life feels auspicious is that I have encountered many authentic Tibetan lineage holders who have kindly shared the teachings of the Buddha.

I am not a scholar, so as a reader you will not get any profound explanation of the Nine Yanas or paths of Vajrayana Buddhism or even well-articulated recollections from the 84,000 teachings of the Buddha. You will be presented with some profound or even pith instructions that I have received from my teachers.

This is not intended to be a self-help book. Obviously, everyone wants to be relaxed and free from stress. Wellness is a 1.5 trillion-dollar industry. On YouTube you can explore self-love guided meditations, relaxation music videos, download positive energy, even learn how to take a spiritual ice bath. Everywhere you look, mindfulness and yoga retreats are offered in tranquil beach towns in Mexico. Usually they include a spa, massage with hot stones, green drinks, and sunrise yoga by the sea. There are thousands of spiritual anxiety pacifiers. This book recounts a different way.

What is a journey into Tibetan Buddhism? It is not a path to reify the ego. It is a path of training the mind and destroying self-clinging. A path of developing wisdom and compassion. You can study and read books which can be helpful, but it really begins with finding a teacher. If you think of someone who is free from cultural norms, conflicting emotions, and habitual patterns, someone who is confident and self-possessed, someone who compassionately works with students, you may get the idea of a teacher. By watching him or her you might even get the idea of what you can become. For 2,600 years the Buddha's teachings have been passed down in an unbroken stream through various oral lineages. What a blessing to encounter and study with a genuine lineage holder.

My aspiration in writing this book is that you might receive some insight into how one can enter the path of Buddha Dharma (teachings). How one can work with the guru.[1] This is the story of my spiritual journey into the heart of Tibetan Buddhism. I think if you had no interest in Tibetan Buddhism or Buddhist teachers you would not be here reading this book.

Over the years I have watched many people with great desire to approach the teacher held back by timidity and fear. Not only new students but also well-seasoned Dharma practitioners. I see these disciples refrain from approaching the teacher, either from discomfort or out of what I consider a false respect or devotion. Many see the teacher as a superhero and as students they are unworthy of presenting themselves. Dharma teachers are heroic and extremely busy, occupied with teaching and all kinds of projects in their mandala. Still, I have never met an authentic teacher who was not approachable.

It is true that the teacher is not your travel agent or marriage counselor and I imagine it is tedious for teachers to be asked about all the mundane personal aspects of your life. You should not be afraid to approach a lineage holder, but you could be afraid of asking questions that are not relevant to your practice or path and unnecessarily wasting the teacher's precious time. Of course, there are times when the guru will ask you about news or politics or how your partner is. I have been asked by one of my teachers if I thought Obama would be elected or how I felt about Trump. I was once asked by the Dilgo Khyentse Yangsi, quite out of the blue on New Year's Eve in Bodhgaya, what I thought about the Russians. I thought he was joking as this was before the invasion of Ukraine. Oddly enough, right after that I ended up at a bar drinking with a large table of Russians.

Guru devotion is an important part of the Vajrayana path. In tantra, three aspects of the guru are often spoken of. The outer guru, who is the guru right in front of you. This is the guru you can relate to. He cracks jokes, tells stories and maybe likes tacos *al carbon* like you. So, what is the outer guru's job? Dzongsar

---

[1] For good explanations of what the guru is you can find much in Chögyam Trungpa Rinpoche's writings and also *The Guru Drinks Bourbon?* by Dzongsar Khentse Rinpoche, Boulder, CO: Shambhala Publications, 2016.

Khyentse Rinpoche has said the guru's job is to utterly destroy your ego. To pull the rug out from under the student. At the same time the outer guru never gives up on you. In the case of the inner guru, the guru's enlightened mind and your mind have become inseparable.

Dzogchen Ponlop Rinpoche puts it another way.

> The guru is like a mirror, nothing more, nothing less.... It simply reflects who you are. Ultimately, what the guru is doing is reflecting your nature of mind. The enlightened mind that you see before you is a reflection of your own true nature of mind.[2]

And the secret guru is no other than the nature of your mind, buddha nature.

The nature of mind is said to be primordially pure from beginningless time. From the Dzogchen point of view, its nature is empty, its essence is clarity or luminosity and it manifests as unobstructed compassion. In Mahamudra terminology, it is called ordinary mind. You might ask why do you need the outer guru if the nature of mind is your real guru? The outer guru teaches you how to progress along the path. It is like being an apprentice to a great cook or a carpenter or an artist. Without the guidance of someone accomplished, someone who has realized the path, it is difficult to accomplish your goal. Also, the outer guru brings blessings from the uninterrupted lineage coming down from the historical Buddha. With the help of these blessings, he points out the nature of mind.

Getting into Buddhism usually involves some uncertainty about the validity of samsara or our world of habitual patterns and projections. If you were totally satisfied with your life, you probably would not be interested in the Buddhist path. This dissatisfaction

---

2   Dzogchen Ponlop Rinpoche. "Song from the Heart: Commentary by Dzogchen Ponlop on Kagyu Mahamudra Supplication." *Bodhi Magazine* Vol 8, no. 2, p. 3, 2007. Translated by the Nalanda Translation Committee under the direction of Chögyam Trungpa Rinpoche. Circa 1975, 1980 by Chögyam Trungpa. Reprinted by special arrangement with the Nalanda Translation Committee, 1619 Edward Street, Halifax, Nova Scotia, Canada B3H 3H9.

with mundane life is what drove me to Tibetan Buddhism. It is difficult to break through the patterns of your life and accept that your ego and the world are not truly existent but just your projections. I never entertained the idea that I could do this without help. So this book is the story of the help and inspiration I have received from my teachers.

I feel blessed, like a stray dog that wandered into a palace. I was able to emerge from the hippy generation of the 70s and encounter the genuine Dharma in the West. In my case, it arrived in the package of Tibetan Buddhism unpacked by Chögyam Trungpa Rinpoche.

Once opening the faucet holding back the teachings of the Buddha it is difficult to resist drinking the water. It is like following a mirage in the desert and finally finding a genuine oasis. My teachers have presented everything I share in this book. I am only passing on their teachings in the tradition of "Thus have I heard...."

Since photography has been so intertwined with my Buddhist path, I share in this book many photographs of great teachers and some of my travels with them. For me, looking at the teacher and his or her activity is almost as important as listening to the teachings. Since the early Trungpa Rinpoche days in the 70s I have been taking photos at retreats and other Dharma events. In more recent times I was fortunate enough to be the primary photographer of His Holiness the 17th Karmapa's first U.S. and European tours.

Most everyone is familiar with Henri Cartier-Bresson's famous quote of capturing a decisive moment. That takes mindfulness of your surroundings. Photography can be a distraction, but photography can also direct one's awareness to "short moments, many times." In higher Tantric teachings, resting in that moment of naked awareness is the essence of the path. I have at times experienced when the teacher is staring at me through the lens a sense of pointing out the nature of mind. I think this can be communicated to others through the portraits I have taken.

I hope you enjoy my journey with teachers, Dharma, and photography. May this book be of some benefit to those who encounter the Dharma.

Introduction

Halifax was cold and gray when we arrived. Kathy and I, along with our six-month-old son Daniel, had flown to Halifax for the Parinirvana of Chögyam Trunpa Rinpoche. Losing our teacher filled our hearts with sorrow. We spent several days going to the house where they placed Rinpoche's body after his death. It was strange to enter the room and see your teacher sitting lifeless in meditation posture on a throne. The last time we had seen him on a throne he was giving teachings. I believe he remained in the state of *tukdam* (a state in which a realized master remains in samadhi after death) for five days. The heart remains warm during tukdam.

For me, the passing of my root teacher brought a deep sense of emptiness and a lack of direction. His teaching offered a life that made sense, a life viewed as the path to awakening. Having this taken away opened a void of uncertainty before me.

Although I was married with three sons and ran a business in Boulder, Colorado, Trungpa Rinpoche had been the heart center of my life. Besides grief, a profound sense of remorse arose. My teacher was dead and I had lost all opportunity to ever speak to him again. I felt regret at not having ever fully exposed myself to him. All those years as his student I had been too shy or embarrassed to be myself around him. Imprisoned in the cell of my ego clinging I could never relax in his presence. His words about not being afraid to be a fool echoed in my mind. Yes, I had been afraid to be a fool, to myself or others. During those gray days in Canada I resolved that whenever the opportunity arose, I would never let fear or shyness impede my approach to the teacher.

How does one come to enter the path of Dharma and find a spiritual guide? Everyone is living out this dream-like existence driven by their own karma and projections. Each person will find their path and encounter their teacher based on their own merit and past actions. I cannot shed any light on how others enter a spiritual path. I only know what came to pass in my life and what brought me to Tibetan Buddhism.

By the age of sixteen, I had become disillusioned with my Jewish upbringing. The Judaism my family lived was more cultural and historic than spiritual. It revolved around holidays, like

Hannukah, Passover, Yom Kippur, and Sukkot. With the exception of Yom Kippur, the holiest day of the year, and Sukkot, a harvest festival, most holidays celebrated historic events. Much of Jewish culture centers around the myth of a chosen people who, for some mysterious reason, God favored. Along with this election and a history of persecution came the idea that Jews must always stick together. My father saw goyim or gentiles as people to be friendly with when passing on the street, or as friends at his bookbinding business, but they were never invited over for dinner. The idea of dating or getting serious with a gentile stressed him. Growing up in our household often felt like living in a private club. Non-Jews were rarely invited to family gatherings.

Sunday school at the conservative synagogue Mount Sinai presented the classic biblical God, both savior and wrathful despot. Jehovah with his long white beard and outstretched arms was either blessing the Israelites or smiting them with horrendous hardships. After escaping Egypt and meandering aimlessly for forty years in the Sinai desert, God delivered them to a promised land. In this land of milk and honey, they were either defending their territory or being conquered. In this conservative version of Judaism I could not find a spiritual path or an authentic teacher. Perhaps if I had been born into a Jewish Orthodox or Hasidic family, my experience of Judaism might have been different.

I began exploring other spiritual traditions. I investigated Sufism, Hinduism, and practices like kundalini, pranayama, and hatha yoga. I read Christian mysticism, the Essenes, the Gnostics, and even the Jewish Kabbalah. In my last year of high school, I came across the book *Meetings with Remarkable Men* by Gurdjieff, an early twentieth century mystic.[1]

Gurdjieff adhered to the belief that there was no solid unified self. Instead, there was a collection of different personalities or selves that one reified into this idea of one enduring and contiguous self. He presented a view of people living in a hypnotic state he called "waking sleep," perceiving reality from a completely subjective point of view. He felt most existing forms of religion had long ago lost their original authentic teachings and now served little or

---

1   George Ivanovich Gurdjieff. *Meetings With Remarkable Men*. New York, NY: E.P. Dutton & Company, Inc., 1969.

no purpose. Gurdjieff taught that through self-remembering "one could realize one's human potential. Years later, I realized how similar Gurdjieff's ideas and what he called "The Work" were to the Tibetan Buddhist teachings.

At Washington University, I majored in Comparative Religion and English literature. I continued to explore mysticism and various spiritual paths. I read books like *The Varieties of Religious Experience* by William James, and the writings of Thomas Merton, Krishnamurti, and Ramana Maharshi. I enjoyed the poetry of William Blake and Walt Whitman. I also read many books on Soto and Rinzai Zen—books by D.T. Suzuki, Alan Watts, and Shunryu Suzuki Roshi. I studied and tried to comprehend the ideas of emptiness, impermanence, and non-self. Unfortunately, it was all very intellectual. I made little genuine connection with the Buddhist teachings of compassion, bodhicitta, or pure perception.

Looking for altered and higher experiences, I experimented with LSD, mushrooms, and peyote. After my third year of college, I decided I needed a break. I traveled west from St. Louis and ended up in Boulder. I made a Mexican friend while camping in the canyon above the town of Boulder. I did not realize at the time that I was just minutes from the home of my future teacher who lived in Four Mile Canyon. My new friend and I drove together to Mexico City.

I spent close to a year in Mexico. For the first few months, I lived in a poor barrio on the outskirts of Mexico City with a yoga teacher, his mother, and his young son. It was a modest house with two bedrooms and a concrete courtyard. They lived an austere life. There was no shower or hot water. Every morning we stripped off our clothes and bathed by pouring buckets of cold water on each other. I practiced hatha yoga in a downtown studio where my friend taught. After a month in Mexico, I contracted a severe case of hepatitis. I wasn't able to eat solid food or get up from my pad on the concrete floor for two months.

After recovering, I traveled to Oaxaca, the land of Maria Sabina. There I had my first experiences with mushrooms and another hallucinogen called *semillas de la Virgin*. One night I ate these seeds of the virgin. I started with a handful. After an hour of not having any extraordinary experience, I consumed more. Disappointed that nothing was happening, I went to bed. In the middle of the night, I suddenly awoke. Everything was radiating and vibrating. Feeling electrified I realized the semillas de la virgin had kicked in.

The door to my room was open. People began passing by dressed with black top hats and sombreros. Their faces were painted white like skeletons with deep dark eyes and red and black lips. They were dressed in bizarre costumes. For a moment, I was not sure if I was awake or dreaming. Then I realized it must be Día de Muertos. This was my first Day of the Dead.

I spent a few weeks in the mountains of Oaxaca then drove to Puerto Angel, a small fishing village on the Pacific coast near Puerto Escondido. Today it is a tourist destination but in 1971 people drove for two hours on a dirt road through the jungle to arrive there. For a few dollars you could live on the playa with a Mexican family, sleeping in a hammock and eating three meals a day. I spent about a month living on the beach smoking pot, contemplating the ocean, and eating *huachinango* (red snapper).

Family in Puerto Angel, Mexico.

I was your typical 70s, undisciplined, self-absorbed hippy thinking he was on the spiritual path. In reality, I was just wasting time. I had no practice, no discipline, and no teacher or lineage I followed. Somewhere buried deep inside was this nagging feeling that this dream-like life was empty and would never be satisfying.

Chögyam Trungpa Rinpoche

Chögyam Trungpa Rinpoche at his home
in Four Mile Canyon, Boulder, CO, circa 1973.

After that year in Mexico, I returned to Washington University to finish my degree. Things had changed. My girlfriend Anne, having felt abandoned by my journey to Mexico, did not want to see me. Life suddenly felt lonely and bleak. I felt the urge to find a path or purpose in life. One day, I came across a book by the Tibetan Buddhist teacher Chögyam Trungpa Rinpoche titled *Meditation in Action*.[1] It is a very concise book, based on talks he

---

1 Chögyam Trungpa. *Meditation in Action*. Boulder, CO: Shambhala Publications, 1970.

gave at Samye Ling, a Buddhist center in Scotland he founded with Akong Rinpoche. In the book, through the story of the life of the Buddha, Rinpoche speaks about the three marks of existence—impermanence, suffering, and egolessness. He explores the six *paramitas* (perfections). The paramitas are associated with transcendent actions that go beyond ego orientation and activities. They are generosity, discipline, patience, energy, clarity, and wisdom.

In talking about the spiritual path, he used analogies I had never come across, like this passage:

> Unskilled farmers throw away their rubbish and buy manure from other farmers, but those who are skilled go on collecting their own rubbish, in spite of the bad smell and the unclean work, and when it is ready to be used they spread it on their land, and out of this they grow their crops... the Buddha says, those who are unskilled will divide clean from unclean and will try to throw away samsara and search for nirvana.[2]

Before this, I had always held the belief that the spiritual path was about purification and that purification was about sorting the dirt and pollution from what was supposed to be the underlying purity. It was liberating to think that one could actually use everything one had ever accumulated to fuel the path. Of course, like most other spiritual seekers I was looking for nirvana or some enlightened state that was far away, full of flashing lights like a spiritual disco. It was revolutionary to think that there was no journey to a distant land of enlightenment and that nirvana was not to be found outside of samsara. It could be right in front of your face, so close, like your eyelashes, so you could not recognize it was your natural state.

It was not just the ideas that Trungpa Rinpoche presented but the way he presented them. He communicated the teaching of the Buddha in a language that was accessible. The very tone and cadence of his words penetrated profoundly and I knew I wanted this person to be my teacher. In the summer of 1973, I went to Boulder, Colorado to find him.

---

2   Chögyam Trungpa. *Meditation in Action*. Berkeley, CA: Shambala Publications, 1970, p.23. Rinpoche recalled this teaching from the *Lankavatara Sutra*.

I ended up at Rocky Mountain Dharma Center where Trungpa Rinpoche was giving a seminar on teachings from the *Tibetan Book of the Dead* and the bardos. The *Tibetan Book of the Dead* is one of the most well known *terma* treasures, or concealed teachings, of the Nyingma school, thought to come directly from the hidden treasures of Guru Rinpoche.

I remember seeing him from a distance as I entered the large tent where the teachings were being held. He looked in my direction. I felt like someone had just stripped me totally naked. My neurosis seemed completely exposed. Strangely, it was this frightening uneasy feeling, this acute awareness of my self-consciousness that convinced me that this was my teacher. I spent the rest of the summer at Rocky Mountain Dharma Center. This was my first experience with longer periods of meditation practice. Here I did my first ten-day solitary retreat.

James Gritz, Rocky Mountain Dharma Center, 1973.

After the retreat, I returned to Boulder and rented a room at Marpa House, a community house filled with students of Trungpa Rinpoche. I had my first interview with Rinpoche at 1111 Pearl Street, then called Karma Dzong. I believe there were around seventy people in the Boulder Buddhist community at that time. When I entered the room Rinpoche was sitting behind a large desk. The window behind him overlooked downtown Pearl Street.

After a few minutes of getting acquainted, I began telling Rinpoche about these repeating experiences I had when taking psychedelics. I explained the experience of seeing what began as a pattern of interlaced lines of light, triangular shapes that were undulating forward and back in the sky. This vortex of light energy would link up through the eyes and join a similar pattern of energy within, creating a deep sense of confidence and relaxation. This external web of light seemed to be the fabric of the universe. I felt since I always had the same experience that this vision was more than just a hallucination or just an ordinary projection of my mind.

When I finished sharing these experiences Rinpoche looked at me and said, "you don't need to always become seduced by the glorious." He banged his coffee cup on his desk and said, "Mahamudra is right here!" This was my first real introduction to Buddhism from a genuine lineage holder. Years later, I realized Rinpoche was pointing out the ordinary mind, the natural state which doesn't need to be sought after as something special, something out there. I am grateful to have encountered such an awakened being who opened the door to the treasury of oral instructions that would continue to guide me for the rest of my life.

I received my first meditation instruction from Trungpa Rinpoche in a small trailer parked in the woods at Rocky Mountain Dharma Center. In those days it served as Rinpoche's office. We sat facing each other on the floor. I began by asking him about a practice I was doing from Krishnamurti. It was a self-inquiry practice of asking "Who am I?" He said, "That is good but you should think of it more as a statement." I'm not sure I completely understood his meaning. Perhaps he was implying that the inherent non-existence of self is not a question.

He then gave me meditation instruction. He said sit up straight and be aware of your body. Now follow your breath. Go out with the out-breath. Don't worry about the in-breath, it will take care of itself and return naturally. Each time you follow the out-breath, rest in space as the breath goes out; there is a gap; then just let the breath return. He told me to let my thoughts just come and go, I didn't need to follow after them. When you find yourself distracted, return to the breath. That was it—very simple. Even though this was a shamatha instruction it laid the foundation for understanding more advanced teachings I was fortunate to receive later in my life.

I think of Trungpa Rinpoche as a Padmasambhava coming to America and transplanting the Buddhadharma by subduing the counterculture of wild, free love, pot smoking, psychedelic hippies. He was the first Tibetan teacher to come with a deep understanding of the Western mind and an impressive command of the English language. Eventually, he dressed undisciplined hippies in jackets and ties. He introduced us to an awareness of head and shoulders, dignity, and precision. He presented the genuine teachings of the Buddha in a straightforward and diligent manner, unadorned by the cultural elements of Tibet.

One of my current teachers, Dzongsar Khyentse Rinpoche, paid this tribute to Trungpa Rinpoche:

> Chögyam Trungpa Rinpoche was a pioneer and igniter of Buddhadharma in the West. Without a doubt, that must have been a challenging task. What Rinpoche has achieved usually takes at least three generations—first introducing, then maturing, and finally stirring things up. Rinpoche managed to do all of this in less than twenty years!
>
> Western disciples might appreciate that what Chögyam Trungpa Rinpoche has done takes great talent. However, as a person from a similar background, I cannot even begin to fathom the amazing courage that he had—this may be more difficult for others to understand.
>
> One of the main challenges in the world today is the inability to understand others' points of view, cultures, and traditions, and therefore being unable to communicate effectively. Rinpoche not only managed to understand the culture and thinking of the West but was then able to interpret Buddhist wisdom, coming up with everything from terms to symbolism and disciplines. He created and communicated all of this incredibly effectively, from the smallest terms to a whole new culture and kingdom, while never diluting the fundamental Buddhist view.

To this day, I think many of us are struggling to teach Buddhism beyond Tibet, beyond the East. We owe him a lot for opening that world.

Twenty years after the passing of Chögyam Trungpa Rinpoche into the parinirvana, I can confidently say as an independent observer that although Rinpoche's students have gone through lots of bumpy roads at times and lots of blissful roads at other times, they have kept his vision, his atmosphere, his smell, and his presence. From my deluded perception, I can only interpret that this must be due to their love and devotion.[3]

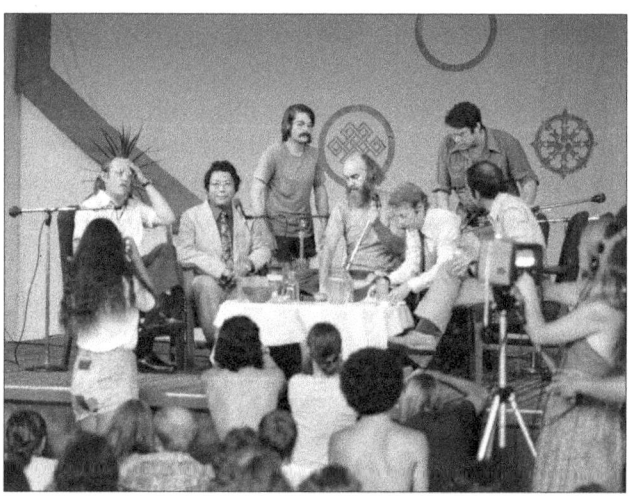

Ram Das and Chögyam Trungpa Rinpoche, Boulder, CO, 1974.

In the summer of 1974, the first Naropa Institute teachings began. They were held in a large warehouse on Arapahoe Avenue known as the Public Service Building. In the first session of the summer, Trungpa Rinpoche taught on the Tibetan Buddhist path and meditation. On alternate evenings Baba Ram Das taught a course on the *Baghavad Gita*.

---

[3] Dzongsar Khyentse. "The Path of Guru Devotion." *The Chronicles of Chögyam Trungpa Rinpoche*, April 11, 2019. https://www.chronicleproject.com/dzongsar-khyentse-rinpoche-2/#:~:text=Ch%C3%B6gyam%20Trungpa%20Rinpoche%20was%20a,and%20finally%20stirring%20things%20up.

Trungpa Rinpoche had invited Ram Das to teach at the first summer Naropa program. Ram Das (born Richard Alpert) was already quite famous in hippy psychedelic counterculture from his book *Be Here Now* and his workshops on conscious aging and dying. His teachings, which included devotional songs to the guru, opening your heart, and of course being here now, drew a large audience. Many went to both teachings. At this stage in my life I was no longer interested in Hinduism and had an aversion to what was designated 'love and light'. I was cynical of what I considered sweet, honey-like devotion to a guru. I found it like Indian incense—overly perfumed and a bit nauseating. I went to some of Ram Das's talks but attended Trungpa Rinpoche's talks consistently. I found his teachings and style stimulating, humorous, and profound. I saw in Trungpa Rinpoche a fearlessness that inspired confidence. He taught based on his realization and understanding of the nature of reality, combining an impressive critical mind with a tender heart of compassion.

In the first summer session, Rinpoche presented the direct teachings from the Buddha. He taught meditation as the way you lived your daily life rather than a mere practice reserved for the zafu. With this approach to practice, based on discipline, one needed to be diligent throughout the day. The path of meditation begins with shamatha and develops through vipassana.

Through exertion one develops a sense of tranquility and awareness begins to permeate your daily life. The formal meditation instruction itself was no different from the instruction I had received directly from Rinpoche. It has nothing to do with getting high or attaining some altered state. By giving space to one's thoughts during meditation one begins to gain freedom from the incarceration of the discursive mind, something which Rinpoche referred to as subconscious gossip. When the mental noise dies down one begins to appreciate sight, sound, smell, and all our sense perceptions. Many teachers use the metaphor of a glass of muddy water. If you stir the water it just gets more cloudy but if you leave it alone the dirt sinks to the bottom.

By dissolving some of the elaborations of ego, the path of shamatha naturally leads to the experience of vipassana—development of insight or clear seeing. It is a sense of expanding into a more panoramic awareness, an open awareness that gives birth to meditation in action. This is the way mindfulness is carried from the cushion into daily life and we experience a direct connection to reality.

Trungpa Rinpoche taught the three aspects of the Buddhist journey—ground, path, and fruition. The ground is that the phenomenal world of compounded things does not truly exist. The external world is no more than a projection of our subjective mind. The path itself brings the realization of this emptiness or shunyata. The realization of emptiness of other and emptiness of self gives birth to enlightenment. With the dawning of enlightenment, you begin to express your innate Buddha nature.

In the second summer session, Trungpa Rinpoche taught a course called The Tantric Journey. In these teachings, Rinpoche explained the Vajrayana path in a simple and direct manner. Besides presenting in detail the path of tantra, Trungpa Rinpoche constantly reminded us of what he termed spiritual materialism. He gave this warning:

> Walking the spiritual path properly is a very subtle process; it is not something to jump into naively. There are numerous sidetracks that lead to a distorted, ego-centered version of spirituality; we can deceive ourselves into thinking we are developing spiritually when instead we are strengthening our egocentricity through spiritual techniques. This fundamental distortion may be referred to as spiritual materialism.[4]

1974 was the year that I took refuge in the Buddha, Dharma and Sangha with Trungpa Rinpoche. The ceremony took place in the shrine room of Karma Dzong. The week before, I cut my long hair and shaved off my beard. I felt I was making a symbolic offering of my ego and sense of identity. In the actual refuge ceremony, there is a point where the teacher cuts a small lock of hair from the head of each refugee. Trungpa Rinpoche said:

---

[4] Chögyam Trungpa. *The Essential Chogyam Trungpa*. Edited by Carolyn Rose Gimian. Boston, MA: Shambhala Publications, 1999, p. 41.

When we take refuge we commit ourselves to the Buddhist path. This is not only a simple but also an extremely economical approach. Henceforth we will be on the particular path that was strategized, designed, and well thought-out twenty-five hundred years ago by the Buddha and the followers of his teaching. There is already a pattern and a tradition; there is already a discipline. We no longer have to run after that person or this person. We no longer have to compare our lifestyle with anybody else's. Once we take this step, we have no alternatives; there is no longer the entertainment of indulging in so-called freedom. We take a definite vow to enter a discipline of choicelessness—which saves us a lot of money, a lot of energy, and lots and lots of superfluous thinking....

You take refuge in the Buddha not as a savior—not with the feeling that you found something to make you secure—but as an example, as someone you can emulate. He is an example of an ordinary human being who saw through the deceptions of life, both on the ordinary and spiritual levels.[5]

---

5   Chögyam Trungpa. *The Heart of The Buddha*. Boston, MA: Shambhala Publications, 1991, p. 74.

James Gritz, Boulder, CO, circa 1973.

I have this image of life before taking refuge with Trungpa Rinpoche. I imagine a lion chasing me through the savanna in Africa. Running for my life I come across this grass hut. I make it inside and slam the door before the lion pounces. Ah, safe and relieved. Then the lion scratches at the door. The hut is not very strong or well-built and the latch on the door is not very secure. The lion is pushing and every time he jumps against the door the walls of this fragile hut shake. I am feeling better than when the lion was chasing me through the open field but now I am paranoid and fearful that the latch on the door might give way and this fierce lion could get in.

This is how I felt about becoming a student of Trungpa Rinpoche. For me, he was the first to offer protection from this wild beast called samsara. He offered an option to the cliches of a life based on following conventional social norms—an option to a cowardly, complacent life in a cocoon of material and psychological comfort. He was the lion pushing on the flimsy structure of ego.

He taught by showing that everything could be brought onto the path. Nothing needed to be rejected. As he says in *Myth of Freedom*, "That is the lion's roar, that whatever occurs in the samsaric mind (the mind of cycles) is regarded itself as the path: everything is workable."[6]

In 1976, Trungpa Rinpoche began presenting the many forms and levels of Shambhala teachings. The Shambhala wisdom is considered the mind terma of Trungpa Rinpoche.[7] On the Shambhala path, the warrior-student has discovered his basic goodness. From the ground of this sanity, the warrior emanates a sense of peace and goodness to the world. One by one, moment by moment, we as warriors can change this setting sun world, as Rinpoche called it, into an enlightened society.

From my limited perspective, the outer form of Shambhala training wraps basic Buddhism into a non-sectarian package. To follow this path, one did not need to take refuge in the Buddha

---

6   Chögyam Trungpa. *The Myth of Freedom and the Way of Meditation.* Boulder, CO: Shambhala Publications, 1976, 71.

7   This is a category of *terma* or hidden teachings discovered within the mindstream of the *terton* or realized master.

Chögyam Trungpa Rinpoche, Boulder, CO
during a Midsummer's Day festival, circa 1977.

or partake in any kind of traditional religious forms. The only difference between the basic level one of Shambhala training and a Buddhist full-weekend meditation practice was the vocabulary. There was no reference to anything Buddhist or religious. "Basic goodness" is a secular way of saying Buddha nature, the unconditioned and awake nature we have always possessed. You might it is the opposite of the Christian idea of original sin.

The *bhumis* or levels of the bodhisattva journey became the path of the warrior. The meditation practice is shamatha without the name. In the typical program, there were two talks a day with the rest devoted to meditation. There was also the opportunity to

Gesar of Ling thangka I purchased in Nepal, 2000.

speak with an experienced student. The Shambhala path begins with basic goodness. The path is the return to this primordial unborn, unceasing condition. It is not the discovery of any new state of illumination. Trungpa Rinpoche's book *Shambhala: The Sacred Path of the Warrior* opens with this passage:

> From the great cosmic mirror without beginning or end,
> Human society became manifest.
> At that time liberation and confusion arose.
> When fear and doubt occurred
> Toward the confidence which is primordially free,
> Countless multitudes of cowards arose.
> When the confidence which is primordially free

Was followed and delighted in,
Countless multitudes of warriors arose....[8]

The Shambhala title of Trungpa Rinpoche is the Dorje Dradul, which means Indestructible Warrior. He introduced many new practices that were revealed to him as terma texts. These included *Letter of the Black Ashe, Letter of the Golden Key that Fulfills Desire, Golden Sun of the Great East,* and the *Scorpion Seal of the Golden Sun.* These teachings were passed on directly from the warrior-king Gesar of Ling, considered an emanation of Guru Rinpoche.

Chateau Lake Louise, Canada, 1979.

In 1979 I attended the three-month Vajradhatu Seminary held at Chateau Lake Louise in Canada. In all, there were thirteen seminaries held between 1973 and 1986. The seminary deepened my understanding of Buddhadharma. It formed the foundation for the path that I have followed.

The seminary began with two weeks of meditation practice followed by an in-depth study of Hinayana teachings from early Buddhism. Hinayana is a Sanskrit term that literally means lesser vehicle or smaller path. The Hinayana path is distinguished from the Mahayana (great vehicle) or the Vajrayana (diamond

---

8   Chögyam Trungpa. *Shambhala: The Sacred Path of the Warrior.* Berkeley, CA: Shambhala Publications, 1984, p. 23.

vehicle) as a Buddhist path aimed at individuals who could leave home and become monks and nuns. And even though the Hinayana included at least 18 early Buddhist schools, the term has sometimes been used negatively to mean an exclusive versus inclusive path. But Trungpa Rinpoche repeatedly said the Hinayana should not be considered an inferior path. From his point of view it makes up the foundation of the Buddhist path. He used the following metaphor. If you are building a high rise and your foundation is not made properly, the whole structure will collapse.

Shamatha meditation practice which is emphasized in all Buddhist practice is the foundation of the spiritual path. It is practice of calm abiding that permeates the path of all yanas. It is also the practice that sets the stage for the practice of Trecho, the main practice of Dzogchen.

We sat through another two weeks of intensive meditation practice before we began the Mahayana study session. Finally, there was a third practice session followed by the Vajrayana teachings. Aside from Rinpoche's teachings we also formed into study groups led by senior students. These discussion groups helped clarify the questions we had regarding the morning teachings.

During most of his life, Trungpa Rinpoche wanted his teachings at the seminaries to remain private, only to be shared with others who had attended seminaries. Later in his life he decided that it was time to make the teachings public. They are published in a three-volume set under the title The Profound Treasury of the Ocean of Dharma. This compilation of talks and seminars edited by Judy Lief presents a comprehensive and three-yana overview of the Buddhist path. Judy Lief summarizes the three-volume work, this way:

> ...the hinayana refers to individual development and the path of the arhat ('worthy one'); the mahayana refers to the joining of wisdom and compassionate action and the path of the bodhisattva ('awake being'); and the Vajrayana refers to fearless engagement and spiritual daring and the path of the siddha ('holder of spiritual power'). The three-yana approach presents

a map of the path based on a student's natural, developmental progression.[9]

At this Seminary, we studied *Lojong*, the fifty-nine slogans on Training the Mind and Cultivating Loving-Kindness.[10] The slogans are included in Atisha's *Seven Points of Mind Training*. Mind training is the process in which we unravel the habitual patterns that support our ego-clinging. The slogans include such advice as "In post-meditation be a child of illusion", "Be grateful to everyone", "Don't be so predictable"; "Don't expect applause"; and one I try to take to heart: "Drive all blames into oneself."

Rinpoche spoke of the Lojong from a Mahayana and Vajrayana point of view relating the practices to sacred outlook, devotion, and the *Maha Ati* (great perfection) teachings. The slogans suggest the proper way of reacting to the phenomenal world. For example, Trungpa Rinpoche explained that the slogan "Whatever you meet unexpectedly, join with meditation" is about dealing with sudden occurrences.

> What comes up is not regarded as a surprise, a threat, or an encouragement, but simply as an aspect of your discipline, awareness, and compassion. If somebody hits you in the face, that's fine, and if somebody decides to steal your Coca-Cola, that's fine too. That may be somewhat naive, but at the same time it is very powerful. It is not just a love-and-light approach. It is more than that. The idea is simply to be open and precise and to know your own territory, so you can

---

9 Chögyam Trungpa. *The Path of Individual Liberation: The Profound Treasury of the Ocean of Dharma, Volume One.* Edited by Judith L. Lief. Boston: MA: Shambhala Publications, 2013. This excerpt is from the Editor's Introduction by Judith L. Lief, p. *xxxix*.

10 Here Chögyam Trungpa Rinpoche interpreted The Seven Points of Training the Mind, a crystalline presentation of Atisha's mind-training teachings. Atisha was the 11th century Indian Buddhist reformer of Tibetan Buddhism whose Lamrim or 'stages of the path' teachings are encapsulated in the Vajrayana classic book *The Lamp for the Path*. See Rinchen Geshe Sonam. *Atisha's Lamp for the Path to Enlightenment.* Translated by Ruth Sonam. First Edition. Ithaca, NY: Snow Lion, 1997.

relate with your own neurosis rather than expanding that neurosis to others.[11]

Relating with one's own neurosis and not spewing it out into the environment and contaminating others is crucial to the bodhisattva path of compassion. After the Seminary, Rinpoche asked me to serigraph a beautifully calligraphed poster of the Lojong slogans. I did this in my silkscreen studio in Boulder.

As we moved into the Vajrayana section of the Seminary, Trungpa Rinpoche explained the commitment we were making when entering the vajra world. He compared entering the Vajrayana to a snake entering a bamboo tube. Once you entered the tube there were only two ways to go. You could move towards giving up your ego clinging, moving in the direction of enlightenment, or continue to reify your neurosis heading in the opposite direction to vajra hell. Vajra hell is a frightening option, a state where your solidified ego cuts you off from any possibility of awakening. It is a place where you are walled off, a place where not even the Buddha could help you. Rinpoche warned us of the dangers of the Vajrayana path. He said,

> The reason you get into vajra hell is that you ignore the warnings you receive from the phenomenal world. You become enormously self-righteous and very selfish. You feel that you are correct, so any warnings are regarded as unnecessary and insignificant. You think it is just your thinking process and your fear that prevents you from doing something. So, you override those strong messages and warnings, thinking, "Oh, that's nothing. I'm still going to do it." With that approach you are actually disrespecting the phenomenal world. That is precisely what ego means: disrespecting the messages of the phenomenal world. You are centralized in yourself, just doing what you want to do, what you feel like doing and you do not pay attention to anything around you.

---

11 Chögyam Trungpa. *The Bodhisattva Path of Wisdom and Compassion: The Profound Treasury of the Ocean of Dharma, Volume Two*. Edited by Judith L. Lief. Boston, MA: Shambhala Publications, 2013, p. 116.

That is the definition of aggression, passion and ignorance all lumped together.[12]

Regarding empowerment (*abhisheka*) Rinpoche has said,

> When the teacher gives the student an empowerment, the student begins to realize and understand a total and utter feeling of authentic sacredness. The mind of the teacher and student meet together to appreciate authentic presence. Authentic means not being influenced by kleshas or second thoughts, and presence means that nothing is by innuendo, but everything is direct. So, in an empowerment, there is direct communication between the student and the vajra master.[13]

Once one receives empowerment a samaya between the vajra master and the student is created. Rinpoche said,

> Samaya principle binds together you; your Vajra master, who is also your lover who loves you; and the teachings, which actually strike so much at your heart. For a long time, you have felt so lonely—lonely without a love affair, lonely with yourself. At last you have a chance not to be lonely, to get into the Vajrayana teachings and be included in some kind of world. Right? It is time for you to pull up your socks or your trousers—or as we say in Tibet, hitch up your chuba. That is the samaya principle, that is being bound together in the parachute. You might ask, "Where are we trying to land?" We are trying to land in the Vajra world. And to come to the Vajra world, you can't actually use any other kind of transportation at all, none whatsoever. The only way students

---

12 Chögyam Trungpa. *The Tantric Path of Indestructible Wakefulness*. Edited by Judith L. Lief. Illustrated edition. Vol. 3. *The Profound Treasury of the Ocean of Dharma*. Boston, MA: Shambhala, 2013, p. 270.

13 Chögyam Trungpa. *The Tantric Path of Indestructible Wakefulness*, 2013, p. 266.

can land in the city or metropolis of the Vajra world is purely by parachuting. Each parachutist has to prove himself with his or her tent and cord and self. Therefore, in turn we can have an enlightened society, whose citizens have actually gone through that process. They actually land that way. Therefore, they become good citizens, because they have gone through that process. They never crawled in. In other words, in the Vajrayana citizenship we do not expect any wetbacks.[14]

At the end of the Seminary Trungpa Rinpoche taught on the levels of Mahamudra and Maha Ati. Mahamudra, Maha Ati, and Dzogchen are different but related trainings. In Mahamudra you train with outer appearances and mainly mindfulness is stressed. In Dzogchen you train with inner *rigpa* (grounding knowledge and aim to relax within awareness. In *The Tantric Path of Indestructible Wakefulness*, Trungpa Rinpoche defines Mahamudra like this:

> Mahamudra means "great symbol," but this does not mean purely experiencing the symbol, and not experiencing the real thing. Instead, in mahamudra the symbol itself is the real thing. When we eat spaghetti, it could be said to be a symbol of Italian food. But we are not eating symbolism; we are eating real Italian food. So, a mudra, or symbol, is itself what it stands for. It is the basic thing, the basic stuff. Things stand on their own. When we say "sunshine," it could be an image, but at the same time, real sunshine is taking place. So mahamudra is a greater vision, a greater understanding of the phenomenal world as it is."[15]

Regarding Maha Ati Rinpoche said:

---

[14] Chögyam Trungpa. "Vajrayana" in 1979 Vajradhatu Seminary educational handout, Lake Louise, AB, Canada, pp.44-45.

[15] Chögyam Trungpa. *The Tantric Path of Indestructible Wakefulness*, 2013, p. 589.

> The maha ati practitioner sees a completely naked world, at the level of marrow, rather than skin or flesh or even bones. In the lower yanas, we develop lots of idioms and terms, and that makes us feel better because we have a lot of things to talk about, such as compassion or emptiness or wisdom. But in fact, that becomes a way of avoiding the actual naked reality of life. Of course, in maha ati there is warmth, there is openness, there is penetration—all those things are there. But if we begin to divide the Dharma, cutting it into little pieces as we would cut a side of beef into sirloin steaks, hamburger, and chuck, with certain cuts of beef more expensive than others, then the Dharma is being marketed. In fact, according to Vimalamitra, the reason maha ati is necessary is because throughout the eight lower yanas the Dharma has been marketed as a particularly juicy morsel of food. The maha ati level is necessary in order to save the Dharma from being parceled and marketed; that is, it is necessary to preserve the wholesomeness of the whole path.[16]

Times have changed. Today, many teachers give advanced Vajrayana, Mahamudra and Dzogchen teachings to students who may not have even taken refuge. Perhaps I am just an old Dharma bum who feels that a Dharma practitioner should have a foundation in the Buddhist path and preliminary practices before being exposed to the highest teaching. Even Trungpa Rinpoche, late in his life, decided his Vajrayana teachings should be published. Some of my current teachers present the highest teachings right from the start. I am grateful for Trungpa Rinpoche's early approach. It enabled me to have an idea of what I was getting into before committing to the Vajrayana.

In his opening talk at Naropa during the founding of the Ngedön School of Higher Learning in September of 1982 Trungpa Rinpoche said this:

---

16 Chögyam Trungpa. *The Essential Chogyam Trungpa*. Edited by Carolyn Rose Gimian. Compiled by Diana J. Mukpo. Boston, MA: Shambhala Publications, 1999, p. 198.

We are inaugurating a new program at Naropa Institute, which will be called the Ngedön School. The establishment of this program is extremely important and powerful. It is modeled on the schools of the Kagyü tradition that have studied and achieved the intrinsic understanding of the Buddhadharma. In the Kagyü tradition, the Ngedön school attained and understood the best of the Buddha's teaching. Therefore, we take great pride in it. Introducing the Ngedön tradition in this part of the world, to you as students, will help tremendously.

Ngedön is a shortened form of ngepi-ton. Ngepa means "certain" and "real"; ton means "further essence." So *ngepi-ton* means "understanding and comprehending fully what Buddha actually meant when he taught the Dharma."

Ngedön can be contrasted with the notion of *trangdön*. Trang means "straightforward"; dön means "meaning," or "essence," as before. We could say that the Buddha first taught us the pointing finger, so to speak, which is trangdön, and after that he taught the reality that the finger is pointing to, which is ngedön. For example, a parent might point to the moon and say to the child, "That is the moon," and the child might think the finger itself is the moon [laughter]. Later on, the child will see that the finger is pointing to something else, which is actually the white disk of the moon itself.

Similarly, trangdön is the early stage in one's understanding. First one has to realize and understand the metaphors and the connections at the trangdön level, and then at the ngedön level one asks, "Metaphors for what? With what? What is metaphoring?" There is an analogy for this in the Vajrayogini practice; if you are completely fascinated by the visualization alone, then you are fascinated by the finger. If you look for what Vajrayogini stands for, what the finger is pointing to, then you begin to understand.[17]

Our lives in Boulder in the 70s and 80s were rich with teachings and opportunities to bring our meditation practice into action. Trungpa Rinpoche showed his love for Japanese culture by forming groups for ikebana (the art of Japanese flower arranging), tea ceremony, and *kyudo* (Japanese Zen archery). I studied kyudo for several years with Shibata Sensei who came to Boulder in 1980 at the invitation of Rinpoche. Rinpoche was also skilled in painting, calligraphy, poetry, and photography. For Trungpa Rinpoche, art went beyond the disciplines that are normally considered art. He taught that one could live his or her daily life as art—cooking, washing the dishes, dealing with business, or doing our laundry. With mindfulness and awareness, all phenomenal existence became a dance. All activities could arise as an expression of basic goodness. Trungpa Rinpoche was a renaissance man, blending art, science, and Vajrayana Buddhism toward the goal of establishing what he called an enlightened society.

Trungpa Rinpoche never seemed to tire of pointing out the importance of sense of humor on the path. It is easy to get too serious and heavy handed with your practice. I must make my offerings, light my candles and incense, sit up straight on my zafu, and so on. Of course, these can be good, but they can also contribute to spiritual materialism if you lack all humor with your practice. Rinpoche said, "A genuine sense of humor is having a light touch: not beating reality into the ground but appreciating reality with a light touch. The basis of Shambhala vision is rediscovering that perfect and real sense of humor, that light touch of appreciation."[18]

On Dharma art, Trungpa Rinpoche said:

> Genuine inspiration is not particularly dramatic. It's very ordinary. It comes from settling down in your environment and accepting situations as natural. Out of that you begin to realize that you can dance

---

[17] Chögyam Trungpa, Opening Talk at Ngedön School or Higher Learning, Naropa University, Boulder, CO, 1982.

[18] Chögyam Trungpa. *The Collected Works of Chogyam Trungpa.* Edited by Carolyn Rose Gimian. Vol. 8. Boston, MA: Shambhala Publications, 2004, p.23.

with them. So inspiration comes from acceptance rather than from having a sudden flash of good gimmick coming up in your mind. Natural inspiration is simply having something somewhere that you can relate with, so it has a sense of stableness and solidity. Inspiration has two parts: openness and clear vision, or in Sanskrit, shunyata and prajna. Both are based on the notion of original mind, traditionally known as Buddha mind, which is blank, nonterritorial, noncompetitive, and open.[19]

Trungpa Rinpoche's unorthodox and controversial lifestyle guided great numbers of students along the path of Buddhadharma. I have also heard of others turned off by his life of drinking and his sexual exploits who left Buddhism altogether. There are many critiques of his behavior that can be found in magazines or on the internet.

I realize there are many unethical and unworthy people with the title guru and the whole modern *tulku* system (of finding and (re)placing reincarnated custodians in Tibetan teaching lineages) is very questionable, full of Tibetan Buddhist egos and strewn with charlatans. Perhaps contemporary gurus should come with a warning label.

For me Trungpa Rinpoche does not fall into this category. I feel that those who never experienced him as their teacher, those who did not live with us in his sangha, have little concept of how his way of acting was a manifestation of his wisdom and insight into western culture. You can always say that this view is merely a way of justifying his behavior, yet I feel no need to justify his behavior. Whether you label his activity "crazy wisdom" or not, I saw an enlightened being, unbound by ordinary conventions. From what I witnessed, his care for his students was always his primary concern. Nonetheless I feel that Trungpa Rinpoche eventually drove himself to death from an excess of drinking. I was not there in Halifax to witness his last years. This early death was a great loss as he could have spread the Dharma for several more decades.

---

19   Chögyam Trungpa. *The Collected Works of Chögyam Trungpa: The Art of Calligraphy*. Vol. 7. The Collected Works of Chögyam Trungpa. Boston, MA: Shambhala Publications, 2010, p. 131.

Khyentse Yangsi Rinpoche considered Trungpa Rinpoche in this way:

> There will be a lot of disagreement with me but he drank sake—that itself was an act of art. He smoked cigarettes—that itself was an act of art. He used a Japanese emperor's golden fan—that itself was an immense teaching of elegance, calmness, wisdom, mindfulness and awareness wisdom—that itself is a piece of art. Everything is a piece of art. Especially this quote, "Victory over war." That itself sums everything up.... I truly feel that nobody can opinionate Trungpa Rinpoche. We should see him as he truly was and how he approached the Dharma and Vajrayana and to all of his students, to all of us in this world. I think people shall remember him as who he was. He was a pioneer and he was a hero, and that itself sums everything up.[20]

I remember a time when I attended a Shambhala training weekend. I had stayed up all night with a female friend drinking sake and making love before the Saturday program began. I went to the program tired and hungover. After sitting for a couple of hours of morning meditation practice while listening to the morning talk, something coalesced in my mind. All tension dropped away. A tremendous sense of fearlessness arose. I remember thinking I had not even realized I carried so much tension in my neck, shoulders, and the rest of my body. This experience of relaxation, confidence, and clarity, lasted about a month. I had been a shy person for years, always feeling uncomfortable in large groups and at sangha events. It was such a relief to be able to move through the world without the preoccupation of what others thought of me, without such a sense of self and other. I felt open and at ease. There was a great simplicity and appreciation of just being in the world.

---

20 Elliott, Mark. "What Trungpa Rinpoche Accomplished: Khyentse Yangsi Rinpoche Reflects on Chogyam Trungpa Rinpoche's Life and Teachings." The Chronicles of Chögyam Trungpa Rinpoche, March 21, 2018. https://www.chronicleproject.com/what-trungpa-rinpoche-did/.

Pith Instructions from my Teachers

One night at a wedding party I was sitting next to the Vajra Regent, Osel Tenzin. We were enjoying a drink as we watched the interplay of people at the party. I turned to him and said, "Is this it? It seems so simple." He looked into my eyes and said, "Yes, this is it."

A few days later I went over to Trungpa Rinpoche's house to take a portrait of him. I walked into the room where he was waiting. The moment he looked at me, the state I had mistaken for some kind of awakening, shattered like tempered glass. Instantly I realized that it was just a temporary experience. The sense of awakening vanished like a dream. There is nothing better than the encounter with an enlightened being to unhinge the illusion of a *nyam* or temporary meditative experience. There is a quote by Milarepa that sums up the difference between temporary experience and real awakening. "Experience (*nyam*) is like morning mist. It disappears, but realization is like space; it is unchanging."[21] Clinging to these temporary experiences can hinder your progress on the path because you can become attached to the sense of awakening. It took me many years to give up the expectation for this state to return. For me this is another reason why the guru

Dilgo Khyentse Rinpoche and Chogyam Trungpa Rinpoche

---

21 Personal notes from Dzogchen Ponlop Rinpoche teachings on "Three Words that Strike the Vital Point," circa 2004.

is so important. I have heard Dzongsar Khyentse Rinpoche say, "The guru's job is to destroy your ego, to dismantle everything, your identity, everything." Chögyam Trungpa Rinpoche was this kind of genuine guru. Rinpoche died on April 4, 1987.

At Rinpoche's funeral on May 26, 1987, at Karmê Chöling in Vermont, Dilgo Khyentse Rinpoche said,

> Trungpa Rinpoche was not an ordinary person. He is a being who came to this earth knowing what he was going to do, how to handle beings according to their capacity. He was born in Tibet, but he spent most of his life in the West, to plant the seed of his vision to create a new society. To further this vision, Trungpa Rinpoche gave many teachings, and the most precious thing is to take to heart all these teachings, and put them into practice. In order to create a new society which shines forth the light of great peace, it's important that each one of us develop this vision from within. The moment we can create this among us, then it will be so easy to manifest it throughout the world.[22]

After Rinpoche's death, a period of great controversy and upheaval began in the Vajradhatu community. There was a power struggle for who would continue as the head of the Shambhala community. Some saw Sakyong Mipham as the rightful heir and others wanted the Vajra Regent Ösel Tenzin. The Sakyong was considered the heir to the Shambhala lineage and the Regent was considered the one who would continue the Kagyu and Nyingma teachings of the Vidyadhara. At this point, the center of the Shambhala community was no longer based in Boulder, Colorado but in Halifax, Canada. Rinpoche's son Sakyong Mipham Rinpoche lived there along with a large sangha of Trungpa Rinpoche students. They had immigrated to Canada when Rinpoche moved there in 1986. After a power struggle lasting two years, his son, Sakyong Mipham Rinpoche, ended up as the head of the Shambhala community.

---

22 Hayward, Jeremy. *Warrior-King of Shambhala: Remembering Chogyam Trungpa.* Somerville, MA: Wisdom Publications, 2007, p. 374.

Even to this day, there is still controversy. There are quite a few older students who feel that Sakyong Mipham Rinpoche is not fulfilling Trungpa Rinpoche's vision.

I have no wish to explore all that in this book. I was never inclined to be a student of Sakyong Mipham Rinpoche. I did not feel a connection like I felt for Trungpa Rinpoche. I did enjoy many of the teachings of the Vajra Regent. As a Western student, I felt he had accomplished a lot, but he was not my guru.

Guadalupe Gonzales Rios

Don Lupe, Tepic, Nayarit Mexico, circa 2000.

Disillusioned with the whole early 1990s Boulder Buddhist scene, Kathy and I dropped out of the Shambhala community. We met a Huichol shaman and curandero, Guadalupe Gonzalez Rios, when he was offering healings in Boulder. He was brought to Boulder by Eliot Cowan, the author of *Plant Spirit Medicine*. Along with Don Lupe, Eliot had been leading pilgrimages to Wirikuta, the sacred land of the Huichol Indians. On these pilgrimages peyote was used as the path to enter the spirit world.

Starting from the time I majored in comparative religion, I was drawn to shamanism and the mystic experience. As I mentioned earlier, I had often explored the world of psychotropic drugs. Through altered states, Shamans entered the unseen worlds of gods and plant spirits. Using these connections they were able to channel healing energy.

If you have read the writings of Carlos Castenada and his apprenticeship to Don Juan you are familiar with the idea of plant spirit allies. Peyote was the ally of Don Lupe.

In the history of Tibetan Buddhism and the Bon tradition hallucinogenic plants had been used as an alchemical elixir to attain realization. I have heard of Amanita muscaria, a psychedelic mushroom being used by yogis in an attempt to achieve enlightenment. Even in the contemporary Vajrayana tradition amrita, which means deathless, is consumed before all empowerments. The Rigpawiki quotes the Thirteenth Dalai Lama as saying "All the siddhis, it is said, including the accomplishment of the vajra body of immortality, come as a result of the qualities of amrita."[1] This nectar is said to heal hundreds of illnesses.

At the time Huichol shamanism appealed to us as a possible alternative to the Buddhist path.

It became obvious to us that Don Lupe was a curandero, a compassionate healer. He was quiet and confident in who he was. We developed a friendship which soon led to a twelve-year apprenticeship. Every year we made two pilgrimages to two different sacred sites of the Huichol Indians.

Don Lupe was born on December 12, 1923, in the Huichol settlement of Carotenes de Cerritos in the state of Nayarit, Mexico. His grandfather, Ines Rios, was a well-known shaman known for having discovered a very strong hallucinogenic solanaceous plant related to the nightshade family. Huichols call it Kieri, *el arból de viento*, or the wind tree. They believe this plant grants the power of penetrating the darkness of the underworld. Huichols believe Kieri can grant the power to heal or to become

---

1   "Vajra body," Rigpawiki, last edited on 14 December 2017 at 20:58, https://www.rigpawiki.org/index.php?title=Vajra_body

a great musician, which brings you closer to the gods. His grandfather was a violinist and played at Huichol ceremonies. Don Lupe had no musical skills. He considered Kieri very dangerous. He believed an apprentice should approach the gods humbly by fasting and making offerings. This had been his path as a young man. When I met him, his commitment was to peyote and the sacred land of Wirikuta.

The Huichol cosmology and creation story is rich in imagery and symbolism. There is grandfather fire (Tatewarí), the instructor of shamans, and the blue deer (Kayumari), the spirit guide who leads the pilgrims to peyote. Huichols show a deep reverence and even fear of their gods. Much of their path comprises pilgrimages to sacred lands and entering a sacred space through fasting, sacrifice, prayer, and peyote.

Don Lupe was an accomplished artist. His yarn paintings portrayed the Huichol path through images of the blue deer, peyote, salamanders, serpents, eagles, healing feathers, and offering candles held by pilgrims traveling to the sacred land known as Wirikuta. For the Huichols, Wirikuta is the center of the universe, not so different from Mount Sumeru for the Tibetans. The mental state of being on pilgrimage is very similar to the Vajrayana idea of sacred world or sacred outlook. The experiences around

Don Lupe yarn art painting representing much of the Huichol Cosmology, with peyote, the blue deer, eagles, candle offerings, and more, circa 1996.

the fire in Wirikuta, taking peyote in the desert near El Real de Catorce, brought insight into a dimension beyond our ordinary karmic perception.

Unlike many Huichol shamans, Don Lupe did not sing or play a musical instrument during our nights in Wirikuta. He instructed us to sit around the fire, stay in our place and be with the peyote. For many, the experience of eating peyote began with vomiting. I am generally not prone to vomiting. For me, the experience started with a powerful surge of energy. This first unsettling power of the peyote would make me feel somewhat out of control. Sometimes I would have to leave the group at the fire and the sounds of my companions retching and go off to sit alone in the desert. I found that if I sat upright and stayed with my breath the uneasiness soon vanished. The stiller and more erect I sat the more the energy of the peyote surging through my body stabilized. This brought a sense of confidence, joy, and wakefulness. The usual feeling of a separate self dissolves and one finds oneself merging into a reality with no clear distinction between self and other. Once settled, I would then return and sit by the fire with the others.

In my journey with peyote, it was difficult to distinguish between outer and inner experience. The energy circulating through the channels of my being would project upon the outside phenomenal world as visions. While others described experiences of grandfather fire or the blue deer, my visions more often came from Buddhist practices I was comfortable with—Guru Rinpoche, Vajra Yogini, or the blue Medicine Buddha.

Don Lupe never taught the stages of the Huichol path in detail. He once told me his job was to lead us on pilgrimage to the sacred sites where peyote itself was the teacher and the entrance to experience the other world. Peyote opened many doors of alternative perception and helped channel what seemed limitless energy. I thought of it as a method for working with the subtle body and training for the bardo of death experiences.

One chilly night, in the desert of Wirikuta, I was standing with Don Lupe with our backs to the fire to keep warm. We were looking up at the stars. I asked him what he had learned from the peyote and what he had experienced in all his years of pilgrimage. He turned to me and said that if I were to share even half of my experience and knowledge you would go crazy on the spot. I

Wirikuta desert, Mexico, circa 1998.

didn't know how to respond to this so I continued to stand with Don Lupe in silence looking up at the heavens, our butts warming from the fire.

A large part of the Huichol shamanic journey involves supplication to a pantheon of deities that are part of the Huichol cosmology. Before leaving on our pilgrimage to Wirikuta or our other pilgrimage site on Mount Picacho we would sit around a fire at Don Lupe's ranch near Tepic. Here the apprentices would make their aspiration and prayers to grandfather fire for what they hoped to accomplish on their pilgrimage. Since many of the apprentices were already therapists in more conventional fields like acupuncture, deep tissue massage, or psychology, most prayed to become more adept in their respective fields. Not being in a healing profession or even knowing if I wanted to become a curandero like Don Lupe, I focused my aspirations on attaining realization and the hope I might then be a benefit to other beings.

On a more mundane level, I made the aspiration that my photography career would integrate seamlessly with my Buddhist path. Don Lupe's wife Pachita kept the fire lit that night at the rancho alive for the duration of our pilgrimage.

Although I was never sure what to make of the Huichol gods and later thought of them as what Tibetan Buddhists called local deities, I would like to share a first-hand experience of the power of the Huichol gods. We always fasted from food and water the day we would approach and arrive at Wirikuta. Once we arrived, we dropped our gear where we planned to spend the night and then began to search for peyote. Hungry, thirsty, and sometimes faint, we wandered in the sandy desert trying to find the elusive plant. In the beginning the peyote seemed to conceal itself from our view. Then a pilgrim would encounter one. After discovering the first peyote others would magically appear. Once we encountered the mother peyote we would return to our campsite with the peyote we had collected and build a shrine to the gods of Wirikuta. We placed the peyote in a large pile with our fletchas (arrows and feathers) surrounding it.

On this one occasion, the offering pile was glowing in the warm light of the afternoon sun. At the time I had black and white film in my Leica camera. I wanted to change to color film. I shot a lot of pictures to empty the roll of black and white. I then changed to color film and continued shooting. Don Lupe turned to face me and said "if you continue taking pictures the gods will put your eye out." With these fierce words I stopped taking pictures.

That night I had similar experiences to what I have already described. The only difference was that when I left the fire circle to take a pee or for a break to look up at the stars, I felt uneasy and threatened. I chanted the vajra guru mantra of Padmashambhava

Yarn art by Don Lupe showing a shaman making prayers around the fire surrounded by other Huichol cosmology, circa 1998.

which seemed to offer a sense of protection. As long as I stayed in my place by the fire I felt at ease.

The next morning two apprentices told me that during the night they had visions of the gods cutting my head off. At the time I didn't think much of it. We had peyote left over from the night. Don Lupe was never happy when peyote remained in the morning. He would insist that we eat all that we had picked. With the fresh memory of nausea caused by consuming the pulpous green cactus no one wanted to have another bite. A few of us mustered up the courage to eat what remained. We then packed up and headed to Real de Catorce. In less than a half hour, I was tripping with the full force of the peyote.

In several cars we traveled up the cobblestone road to the old silver mining mountain town of Real de Catorce. Along the way we pulled over to enjoy the view of the desert valley below. Returning to the car I looked down at the cobble stones and saw what appeared to be glowing translucent ancient Mayan or Aztec designs inside the stones. I asked two of my friends if they saw what I was seeing but they did not. I assumed it was just a hallucination. We continued up the road and through the tunnel that ended in town. We then found hotel rooms.

I woke up in the middle of the night to go to the toilet. I'm not sure what happened but my wife heard me moan and found me on the floor of the bathroom in a pool of blood. I must have passed out and hit my head on the doorknob on the way to the floor. My left eyebrow had a large split. There was nothing we could do at the time so we went back to bed. The next morning when I woke there was a scorpion on the wall a foot above my head.

We went into town to find a doctor who could stitch my eyebrow. The only doctor's office was above a corner grocery. We climbed the stairs and entered a small office. A young woman sat in the cluttered space. I noticed videos for sale on a bookshelf behind her. I wondered if she had any medical training. She left the office by a side door and returned with a metal cart of tools and bandages sterilized and neatly arranged. She cleaned the wound and sewed it closed.

After leaving the doctor's office we joined some of our fellow pilgrims for breakfast. During the meal a young girl entered the restaurant and asked if we would like to hear the story of Real de

Catorce. The village of Real de Catorce is nestled on the side of a mountain, in the Sierra de Catorce range, one of the highest plateaus in Mexico. The name itself means the Royal Four, named after 14 Spanish soldiers ambushed by the indigenous Chichimeca warriors. Real de Catorce had once been a thriving silver mining town but became a virtual ghost town after the price of silver plummeted in the 1900s. For years the only people that visited the town were devotees coming to visit the Parish of Immaculate Conception where there is an image of St. Francis, or Huichol pilgrims who came to leave offerings at the sacred site above the town called Cerro Quemado. This is considered the birthplace of Grandfather Fire. At one point during the girl's story she said that in ancient times the stones that make up the road to Real de Catorce were inscribed with silver-colored Indian designs. Maybe, the peyote had the power to open windows into the past.

When we made our pilgrimages to Real de Catorce there were only a few hotels and restaurants. Today, it has become a haven for peyote tourists or bicyclists and runners who come to train at an altitude of almost 9,000 feet. After breakfast we started the long journey back to Tepic. I felt ill during the whole ride back. Once in the bed of our hotel room in Tepic I felt someone had pulled a cork from my side and all my energy was escaping like air from a balloon. I thought I might die and asked Kathy to go get Don Lupe. When he entered the room he glared at me with eyes of recrimination and said, "See, I told you the gods would give you a big golpe (bashing)." It was because I had taken pictures so thoughtlessly without even asking their permission. He worked his magic with his feathers and spit and the next day I felt much better.

Besides our yearly pilgrimages to Wirikuta there was another sacred site we visited. As apprentices we had the choice of making

The way to Mount Picacho, Near Tepic, Nayarit, Mexico, circa 1998.

one or two *compromisos* (commitments or obligations). One was to Wirikuta and the peyote. Our other pilgrimage was to the "arbol de viento", the wind tree. This pilgrimage did not involve any peyote. This pilgrimage involved climbing Mount Picacho, about one-hour drive from Tepic, Nayarit. The Huichols believed the spirit of the wind tree lived here. The commitment to climb Mt Picacho and visit the wind tree as an apprentice was considered dangerous and was therefore optional. Many Huichols are afraid to go there because they say the spirit is unforgiving and any commitment made to the wind tree that is broken could end in sickness or death.

The climb up Picacho was arduous. We left early in the morning and arrived just before nightfall. In the beginning, Don Lupe permitted us to eat some oranges on the way up. He considered his gringo apprentices too weak to make the journey as he did—fasting from both food and water. In the years that followed, he insisted that we didn't even eat the oranges. It was the most strenuous climb I had ever taken. Arriving at the top we collapsed on the small flat area where we would spend the night.

I looked around but didn't see the much-anticipated wind tree. Don Lupe took me to the precipice of the mountain and said look down. I looked but still didn't see the wind tree. "There," he said, pointing to a very tiny branch with a few leaves protruding out the side of the mountain. Wow, I thought. Climbing all day in the heat, dying of thirst only to find this tiny branch he called the wind tree. Apparently, it was not the size of the tree that mattered but the power of the spirit.

Don Lupe took the spirit-power seriously. The story I remember hearing from Don Lupe was that a boy wandering in the mountains became lost and was unable to return to his home. Eventually he died and was reborn into this tree on the side of the mountain. It is said that the tree has great power to grant one's wishes. I am not sure what or if there is a connection to Kieri or the wind-tree I spoke of earlier that is reached through eating a psychoactive plant. According to Don Lupe, praying in earnest to the spirit and following your commitment will lead to one becoming a very skilled healer. Other Huichols make the trip up Picacho to have their wishes granted, like enhancing their skill as musicians. On one of our pilgrimages, we encountered a group of musicians at the top who may have made the climb for just this purpose.

The Wind Tree, Near Tepic, Nayarit, Mexico, circa 1998.

To illustrate the power of the wind-tree and warn us about a commitment to apprentice to this spirit-god, Don Lupe recounted the story of an old friend of his, Juan Negrín. I have no idea if this story is true or a tale Don Lupe used to illustrate the wrathful aspect of the wind tree. Juan Negrín was the Co-Founder and Executive Director of Wixárika Research Center. He was deeply involved with Huichol culture. For a time, he was the curator of the Museum of Guadalajara and a patron of Don Lupe, purchasing and exhibiting several of his yarn paintings. According to Don Lupe, his close friend Juan made the trips up Picacho to the wind tree as an apprentice. For Don Lupe, one of the commitments of the apprentice was absolute fidelity during the first six years of the

Huichol Musicians by the shrine on top of Mt. Picacho, Nayarit, Mexico, circa 1997.

apprenticeship. As he told the story, his friend, who was married, once visited the island of Cozumel where one night, under the influence of alcohol, he slept with another woman. After this, Don Lupe said he contracted an illness. He became so gravely sick that he couldn't eat and began withering away. Apparently, he recovered and outlived Don Lupe because I read that Juan Nigrin died on August 28, 2015, after a yearlong hospitalization for epilepsy. Whether true or not Don Lupe told this story to illustrate the unforgiving power of the wind-tree.

It was around the fifth year of our apprenticeship in 1998 when Don Lupe sprung some surprising news. He said that after the sixth year or what he called going up we were to sacrifice a bull or a deer to Grandfather Fire. While I had confidence in Don Lupe's ability to heal many ailments and guide us on the Huichol path, I began doubting the validity of the path itself. My doubts were not only due to the new revelation of animal sacrifice. I felt that shamanism was not a genuine path to enlightenment but was more oriented towards manipulating the phenomenal world and accumulating individual power.

Jumping ahead in this story, after returning to Buddhism I still felt the need to complete the apprenticeship. I asked two of my Buddhist teachers, Dzongsar Khyentse Rinpoche and Jigme Khyentse Rinpoche, how I could complete my Huichol commitment without making the required animal sacrifice. Independently, they offered me the same advice. They suggested making a *torma* in the form of a bull or deer and offering that to the Huichol gods. In 2000 in Boulder, before my last pilgrimage with Don Lupe, I made a torma in the shape of a deer. My wife Kathy also made a torma to complete her apprenticeship. We took these tormas on our final trip to Wirikuta. I was uncertain how Don Lupe would react but he made no comment about our tormas. While at Don Lupe's ranch in Las Pilas another apprentice, Jack, had arranged to have a bull sacrificed. While very conflicted I sat with the others around the fire that night. I prayed for the bull and also that my torma offering would be accepted and let me finish my compromiso. It was a difficult night for two people who had taken refuge in the Buddha, Dharma, and Sangha and made the commitment not to cause harm or suffering to other beings.

The night we arrived in Wirikuta we offered candles. It was a very windy night which made it difficult to light the candles and keep them lit. I placed mine behind a rock outcrop with the torma and was able to light the candle. Most of the candles blew out in the wind, however mine burned down to the bottom. I took this as a sign that the gods had accepted my torma offering.

As I was saying, in the fifth year of the apprenticeship, I had already returned to the path of Buddhadharma. One day in a store in Fort Collins, Colorado, I was talking to a friend who was a Tibetan translator and the ex-wife of my friend Steve who had been accompanying us on our trips to Wirikuta. I mentioned I was looking for a living teacher. She said why don't you go to Nepal and check out Tsoknyi Rinpoche, a son of the great Dzogchen master Tulku Urgyen Rinpoche. He is great at giving the pointing out instructions, the method given by a skilled teacher that leads to recognizing the nature of mind, or at least planting the seed that may mature into this awareness.

A short time after this I ended up flying to Kathmandu to visit my son Rishone, who was there on a study-abroad program with Naropa University, and also to see if I could meet Tsoknyi Rinpoche. On the airplane, I had a dream of meeting him. In this dream, I was waiting with a group of other students in the living room of his house in Swayambhu. It seemed to take forever for him to come downstairs and I was growing increasingly impatient. Finally, he came down. When the appropriate moment arose, I ap-

After Guadalupe Gonzales Rios, in Nepal

Boudhanath Stupa, Kathmandu, Nepal, circa 2000.

proached him and introduced myself as an old student of Trungpa Rinpoche. He looked at me and said, "Introduce him to me." At that point, I awoke from the dream.

In 2000, after arriving in Kathmandu, I made my way to Tsoknyi Rinpoche's house. The path to his house began near the Swayambhu Stupa. It was a long hike up a steep path on a hot sunny day. I arrived at his house covered in sweat. It was a surprise to see how similar it was to the house in my dream. A servant informed me that Rinpoche was in Bhutan visiting one of his teachers. That was very disappointing.

I returned to where I was staying in a small room in a guest house that faced the Boudhanath Stupa. The following day, while having a breakfast of cinnamon banana oatmeal in a nearby restaurant I noticed an advertisement for Chökyi Nyimas's Shedra, a school for the in-depth study of Tibetan Buddhism. I knew he was Tsoknyi Rinpoche's older brother so I decided to pay him a visit. When I arrived, someone escorted me to a room where I found Rinpoche giving meditation instructions to a group of new students. I sat down and waited until everyone left. I then told him I had been a student of Trungpa Rinpoche and that I was looking for a living teacher.

After some discussion he told me I should visit Tenga Rinpoche. He said he was a very accomplished teacher and was close to Trungpa and many of his students. I knew Tenga Rinpoche from his visit to Boulder in 1985. Tenga Rinpoche had always been close to the Vajradhatu community.

That afternoon I went to see Tengpa Rinpoche at Benchen monastery in Swayambhu. When I arrived, he was in the central compound, surrounded by a group of young monks. Children were holding his hands as he walked. They followed him around like a brood of ducks. It was touching to watch how much they loved him. I wanted to approach him but he went up to his room before I had a chance.

I spoke to a monk about meeting with him. I waited for about an hour and then was led up to his room. He was sitting on his bed when I entered. The monk stayed with us to translate. I told him Trungpa Rinpoche had been my teacher and that now I felt I needed a living teacher. He said that Trungpa Rinpoche was a great teacher and that if you had enough faith and devotion in him you didn't necessarily need a new teacher. If, on the other hand, you still feel unclear about the path and feel you need guidance then it would be good to find another teacher.

Even though Tengpa Rinpoche was a great master and friend of Trungpa Rinpoche, I was looking for a contemporary teacher who spoke English and spent more time in the West like Trungpa Rinpoche. I remembered when Tenga Rinpoche visited the Rocky Mountain Dharma Center to give teachings. At one point he chanted Lama Khyenno with a beautiful heartfelt tune. His devotion had moved me. I asked if we could chant that together. The translator left and Rinpoche pulled out a small tape recorder. He turned it on and it played the melody of the first two lines of the chant known as "Calling the guru from afar."

Lama khyenno, lama khyenno
drinchen tsawey lama khyenno
Kind root guru, think of me.
Essence of the buddhas of the three times....

We chanted these lines over and over again.

Children at the central gompa of Benchen Monastery,
Swayambhu, India, 2000.

Back in the central gompa a group of children saw my Leica camera hanging from my shoulder and came up and implored me to take their picture. I took this picture before leaving the monastery.
The next day I went to Shechen, the Monastery of the late Dilgo Khyentse Rinpoche. Dilgo Khyentse Rinpoche was one of the greatest Tibetan Buddhist masters of the twentieth century. He was the holder of many teachings from all the Tibetan Buddhist schools and passed on the empowerments for these teachings to many of the prominent contemporary teachers. He was one of the principal teachers of all my teachers.

At Shechen, I met the monk Matthieu Ricard for the first time. He told me he was busy for about an hour but I should come up to his office after that. To pass the hour he suggested I pay a visit to a shrine room where there was a life-size statue of Khyentse Rinpoche. There was no one in the room when I entered. The statue was incredibly realistic. A powerful peacefulness pervaded the room.

Shechen Monastery, statue of the late Dilgo Khyentse, 2000.

I sat and meditated in front of his statue for a while and then went to visit Matthieu. He showed me the project he was working on—archiving the photos from the life of Dilgo Khyentse Rinpoche. We developed an instant friendship based on our common interest in photography. Later that day, Matthieu took me to see Trulshik Rinpoche.

Trulshik Rinpoche is one of the heart sons of Kyabjé Dilgo, Khyentse Rinpoche, and Kyabjé Dudjom Rinpoche. Like Dilgo Khyentse Rinpoche, Trulshik Rinpoche was also one of the most important Nyingma masters of modern times. He was also an important teacher to most of my current teachers and many of the

Trulshik Rinpoche, circa 1980.

younger tulkus of the 21st century. When we entered the room, he was sitting on a throne. His awake and compassionate presence permeated the room. My first thought was that he looked like Trungpa Rinpoche. When I mentioned this, he told me it was just my devotion. I think it was the great similarity of their confidence and compassion that made me see him that way.

Matthieu and I sat down in front of Rinpoche. He began teaching on the nature of mind. This was surprising since my experience of meeting great teachers was that they usually began by giving teachings on subjects like bodhicitta and compassion. Since Trulshik Rinpoche was speaking in Tibetan, Matthieu translated, telling me he would remember the teachings and recount them later, so I didn't take notes. Unfortunately, this never happened. I never had another opportunity to see Trulshik Rinpoche. He passed away at the age of 87 on 2 September 2011. He remained in tukdam for three days in his monastery in Kathmandu.[2]

---

2 From Rigpawiki we learn that tukdam (*thugs dam*) is an honorific term for meditative practice and experience that is frequently used to refer to the period following the death of a great master, during which time they are absorbed in luminosity. Rigpawiki, last edited on 24 January 2021, at 21:34, https://www.rigpawiki.org/index.php?title=Tukdam

Jigme Khyentse Rinpoche

Jigme Khyentse Rinpoche, circa 2001.

When we returned to Shechen Monastery in 2000, Matthieu pointed to Rabjam Rinpoche's quarters and informed me Jigme Khyentse Rinpoche was staying there and suggested that I try to meet him. The next day I returned to meet him. A monk came to the gate and informed me Jigme Khyentse Rinpoche was not available. I returned the following day. The same monk came to the gate again and gave the same response to my request to see Rinpoche. On the third day after receiving this response again, I gave the monk my business card with a note on the back of the card saying I was a former student of Trungpa Rinpoche and would like to meet Rinpoche and asked the monk to please give this to Rinpoche. He returned a short while later and told me Rinpoche would see me.

Entering the patio, I found Rinpoche was having lunch with his wife Ingrid. He invited me to sit down. I found his smile mesmerizing and full of compassion. I think I fell in love with him at that moment. Rinpoche's English was perfect and his knowledge and insight about the Dharma was impressive. We talked for most of the afternoon. At one point, walking through the garden area I asked Rinpoche about the nature of mind. I don't remember his exact words, but his response was something like "I don't even know my own thoughts or emotions, let alone the nature of mind." With these words he sidestepped any direct discussion using the words nature of mind.

I don't remember that much of our long conversation that day. However, I remember that right before I left, after a long dialectic discussion Rinpoche looked at me and said, "so how is your mind any different than the mind of the guru?" At that instant, my mind stopped and I had nothing to say. I had no idea how to answer that question. I believe the gap he created in my mind at that moment may have been his unique version of pointing out the nature of mind.

Rinpoche kindly invited me to come back, if I liked, to do the Riwo Sancho Sang offering with him in the mornings. The Riwo Sancho, also called "the mountain smoke offering" was one of the most widely practiced smoke offerings in Tibet. It was a cherished practice of Dudjom Rinpoche (one of Jigme Khyentse Rinpoche's teachers). I came back every morning for the rest of my stay in Nepal. Through sitting with him on the patio those mornings, doing the smoke offering practice, and conversing about Dharma, my connection with Rinpoche deepened.

One afternoon I asked Rinpoche for the *lung* (oral transmission and permission to practice a certain text) for the *Rain of Blessings*, a common guru yoga practice done in both the Kagyu and Nyingma lineages composed by Mipham Rinpoche and based on the seven-line prayer to Guru Rinpoche. It had been practiced by many in Vajradhatu sangha either as a daily or feast practice. I had the text with me and although it was a practice I liked I couldn't remember ever getting the reading transmission.

Jigme Khyentse Rinpoche said before giving me the reading transmission he wanted me to go from temple to temple in Boudha lighting as many butter lamps as I could. While lighting the offering candles I was to recite the seven-line prayer. Every monastery in Kathmandu has a room dedicated to butter candles where you pay by the candle to make offerings. I walked from monastery to monastery lighting all the available candles in each one.

Offering candles, Boudha temple, 2000.

The excursion was a magical one. I felt like I was walking in a waking dream surrounded by devotion. After completing the candle offerings, I did kora around the Boudha Stupa and then walked back to Shechen monastery. At one point, while walking through a small alley, I realized an old Tibetan man was walking next to me carrying a rolled-up Thangka. I looked over at him and we walked together for a while. The old man unrolled a part of the old Thangka he was holding, revealing a painting of Milarepa. He didn't indicate he was selling it. He just opened it and closed it again and went on his way. There was a dreamlike quality to wandering through Boudhanath that night. I felt like I had been walking through a cloud of blessings. Returning to Shechen, I went to see Jigme Khyentse Rinpoche. I sat down in front of him and he gave me the reading transmission.

Before leaving Kathmandu I wanted to offer Jigme Khyentse Rinpoche a gift, a symbol of some bond for the future. After searching in stores all day I found a silver offering cup I thought would make an appropriate offering. Just before I left I offered it to Rinpoche and asked if he would be my teacher. He said he wasn't

Pith Instructions from my Teachers

Matthieu Ricard, Jigme Khyentse Rinpoche, and James Gritz, Kathmandu, 1998.

a teacher and had no students and told me I should keep the cup.

I have not spent as much time with Jigme Khyentse Rinpoche as I would like, but the time I have spent in his company has been precious. Jigme Khyentse Rinpoche is the son of the late Kangyur Rinpoche who was a great master and terton and one of the first masters to teach Tibetan Buddhism to Western students. He was Matthieu Ricard's root guru. Jigme Khyentse Rinpoche's other teachers include Dilgo Khyentse Rinpoche, Dudjom Rinpoche, Trulshik Rinpoche, Tenga Rinpoche, His Holiness Sakya Trizin Rinpoche, Dzongsar Khyentse Rinpoche and his brother Tulku Pema Wangyal Rinpoche. Both Dilgo Khyentse Rinpoche and His Holiness the 16th Karmapa recognized Jigme Khyentse Rinpoche as an incarnation of Jamyang Khyentse Chökyi Lodrö.

The next time I saw Rinpoche was in Bodhgaya, India, in the winter of 2000. He was there teaching along with Rabjam Rinpoche and Dzigar Kongtrul Rinpoche at Shechen Monastery. His teachings on impermanence continue to haunt me. In one talk he said,

> Make impermanence your post-meditation practice. The outer universe with all its immeasurable beings, even great realized beings are impermanent. This world is not permanent. Take refuge whenever you get distracted and bring the mind back to the

Jigme Khyentse Rinpoche, Rabjam Rinpoche, Dzigar Kongtrul Rinpoche, Rajgir, India, 2000.

thought of impermanence. When we realize how impermanent things are, just sit and let our mind take it in. When we meditate on impermanence, it is good to know what we are doing—we are applying the thought of impermanence to our belief that everything is real, solid, and unchanging. We have to give up wrong views, and an improper attitude towards ourselves and others—that everyone is everlasting.[1]

I was able to spend afternoons in Rinpoche's room at Shechen with several others and also on occasion around the Mahabodhi Temple. Sitting there one evening by the bodhi tree he told me to make impermanence my post meditation practice.

One afternoon I went shopping for a mala at the many mala stalls in Bodhgaya. I brought one back to Jigme Khyentse's room in Shechen monastery and asked him if he would bless it. He took one look at it and said he wouldn't bless it. If I wanted his blessing I would need to find another mala. I purchased a second mala and brought that to him. Again, he refused to bless it. I went and

---

1 Personal notes from Jigme Khyentse Rinpoche, Rabjam Rinpoche, Dzigar Kongtrul Rinpoche teachings at Shechen Tennyi Dargyeling Monastery, Bodhgaya, India, 2000.

Pith Instructions from my Teachers

My mala beads.

purchased a third bodhi seed mala from a very handsome Muslim man on a side street not far from the temple grounds. I brought this one back to Rinpoche and not only did he bless it, he also tied a beautiful tassel that runs through the guru bead. He told me that the mala beads were light colored and that the tone would deepen with time and practice. He also told me not to wear it around my neck and that I should keep it in my pocket. Rinpoche was a staunch believer that Dharma practice and objects should not be flaunted in public advertising that you are spiritual.

Years later when Rinpoche came to my house in Boulder he looked at my mala again. It had aged and darkened somewhat but perhaps feeling that it was not dark enough he rubbed some oil on it. I still have this same mala today more than twenty years later. It has been blessed by all my teachers including His Holiness the 17th Karmapa.

There is much written about the symbolism and significance of malas. Bodhi in Sanskrit means enlightenment and bodhi seed malas are said to remove negative energies and enhance meditation practice. A mala made from bodhi seeds can be used in both peaceful and wrathful practices and accomplishes all dharmas.

During his talks at Shechen Monastery Rinpoche spoke on the importance of realizing impermanence many times. In one of his teachings in Bodhgaya, he said:

> For the world to function it is not necessary to have a belief that it is real or permanent. There is a discrepancy between how things are and how we see them. If I am convinced that all phenomena are impermanent, I am convinced that my distractions will be reduced. We have to give up wrong views, and an improper attitude toward others, that everyone is everlasting. There is a discrepancy between how things are and how we see them. We know everything is impermanent but we would rather see it as permanent.[2]

I met with Jigme Khyentse Rinpoche a few more times in Colorado. On one occasion he was staying at Dzigar Kongtrul Rinpoche's practice center, Phuntsok Choling, in the mountains just west of Boulder. Rinpoche came to visit Kathy and me at our home up Flagstaff Mountain. He arrived with Ingrid. We fixed lunch. A couple of hours later a translator and student of Dzigar Kongtrul Rinpoche arrived and we went out on the deck and did the Riwo Sancho Sang offering practice. Together they translated the Tibetan text of the Riwo Sancho into English. I still use the now well-worn copy of the practice we printed that day. Before he left, I once again offered Rinpoche the silver offering bowl I had purchased in Kathmandu all those years ago. This time he accepted the bowl. When offering a bowl like this it should be filled with something like butter. I think I added fruits and nuts.

Rinpoche came to Colorado again to visit a dying student of Dzigar Kongtrul Rinpoche. That evening Kathy and I had dinner with Rinpoche and Ingrid at a vegetarian restaurant in Denver. Rinpoche has always been a strict vegetarian.

---

[2] Personal notes from Jigme Khyentse Rinpoche teachings, Shechen Tennyi Dargyeling Monastery, Bodhgaya, India, 2000.

One day, I received a surprise phone call from Ingrid at my house in Colorado. She said she and Rinpoche were in the Denver airport with a layover and if I wanted to see him, I could come down. Kathy and I jumped in the car and drove to the airport, about an hour away. When we got to the airport, there was confusion about where to meet them. We wasted a half-hour before hearing our names announced on the intercom directing us to where Rinpoche and Ingrid were waiting. By the time we found Rinpoche and Ingrid, there was little time to talk. Before walking Rinpoche to the security line, I asked him for his blessing. He said he would pray to Guru Rinpoche on my behalf. Whatever he did I remember being in a calm state of joy and elation for the rest of the day.

Standing in the security line with Rinpoche I told him how I wished I could spend more time with him. He mentioned a project he was just beginning with his brother Tulku Pema Wangyal Rinpoche in Portugal. His vision was to have a place for students to practice in retreat, an organic garden, and a common kitchen. His deceased mother had a house and property in the mountains of Serra de Monchique in the Algarve. He mentioned other details I no longer remember. Just before parting, he told me he would be teaching in San Francisco the following week and I was welcome to come.

I went to San Francisco. The first teaching took place in a private house in Oakland. The second teaching on Sunday was in the elaborately decorated shrine room of Orgyen Dorje Den. In the shrine hall, there were impressive golden statues of the Buddha and Padmasambhava.

During his teachings, Rinpoche investigated impermanence and what is real in our lives on the Buddhist path. He asked, "What percentage of our spiritual path is a pacifier?" A provoking question I had never given much thought to. He said, "If our spiritual path is a pacifier, we should investigate further.... The Buddha taught the truth of suffering to wake us up from the culture of pacifiers. So many pacifiers keep us asleep." Rinpoche continued, calling our iPhones and Blackberries sophisticated pacifiers. He referred to our careers, our studies, and the degrees we develop as pacifiers.

> When we meditate, [he said,] it is important to see if
> we are building on something that will really wake us

Jigme Khyentse Rinpoche, Orgyen Dorje Den, circa 2010.

up. If all the accouterments of our practice [pointing to the bell and dorje in front of him], our teachers, the Buddha, and the Dharma are treated as a pacifier they will function as a pacifier. It is important to see this, so that in the end we don't blame the Buddha and Dharma, telling ourselves it doesn't work.

How is the Buddha going to help me? How is the Dharma going to help me? Why is the Buddha talking about suffering—the thing we are trying to cover up. The first truth of suffering is that all component things are impermanent. Yet it is so hard to accept this truth. Is eternal permanent happiness possible? How do we relate to our own experience of wanting happiness, not wanting to suffer?[3]

He went on to say that we are looking to solidify everything and make it permanent: our relationships with loved ones, our jobs, and even our practice. Permanence and clinging seem to be synonymous. There is a line from *Flight of the Garuda* that goes something like "If you don't fixate on whatever arises how can there be a cause of going astray?"[4] Fixating on whatever arises in our

---

3   Personal notes from Jigme Khyentse Rinpoche teachings, Orgyen Dorje Den, 2010..
4   *The Flight of the Garuda* is one of the sacred texts of the Dzogchen

thoughts or in our life seems to be another way of trying to make things solid and permanent.

On Saturday night a small group of students accompanied Rinpoche to San Francisco's giant Westfield mall. Together we circumambulated this modern temple of materialism. It was like a dream and I thought back to years ago when I was circumambulating the Great Stupa in Bodh Gaya with Rinpoche and he told me to make impermanence my post-meditation practice. At one point we found ourselves in the Sharper Image store investigating the plethora of high-tech pacifiers. Life is such a dream. One day we are prostrating where the Buddha attained enlightenment and on another, we are receiving teachings in a shopping mall. It teaches us that sacred outlook is not limited to sacred sites like Bodhgaya.

Recently I attended some of Rinpoche's teachings in Portugal. In June 2016 I went to a teaching and empowerment that HH Sakya Trinzen Rinpoche gave in Lisbon. The primary reason I went was to see Jigme Khenytse Rinpoche.

I returned again in November and attended Rinpoche's shamatha retreats along with some other teachings. He taught along with his brother Pema Wangyal Rinpoche and Khenpo Pema Sherab Rinpoche.

Jigme Khyentse Rinpoche often starts with the fundamental teachings of the Buddha. These teachings, though they may not be as enticing as the so-called higher teachings of Mahamudra and Dzogchen, are also profound and comprise the foundation of the path. In Portugal, Rinpoche started with the first noble truth.

> What is suffering? It is the cycle of unpleasant experiences that are the result of deluded actions based on the deluded view. Of course, to think of the suffering of samsara will bring some sadness in our mind. Thinking of the "suffering of suffering" will bring sadness to our mind. Thinking of the "suffering

---

teachings. It was written by an 18th century nonsectarian itinerant Tibetan yogi, Shabkar Tsogdruk Rangdrol. One of the most accessible modern translations is Keith Dowman's text, *The Flight of the Garuda: The Dzogchen Tradition of Tibetan Buddhism.* 2nd ed. Somerville, MA: Wisdom Publications, 1994.

of change" will reduce our attachment and thinking of "all-pervasive suffering" of compounded nature, we will have the wish to be free from samsara. So, that is why contemplating the suffering of samsara is something essential to our path. Not because we need to exercise our pain, but more to develop the proper renunciation, the proper wish to be free, then contemplating the suffering of samsara is considered very important.[5]

In May of 2019 I traveled to France to attend a *drupchen* (meditation retreat) and a certain White Tara empowerment I needed for a sadhana practice I wanted to do.

Tara appears as a female deity and is visualized in many Buddhist practices and pujas. There is a famous practice of twenty-one praises to Tara. She is the liberator that offers protection from all obstacles on the path, long life, and freedom from fear. She is considered the female counterpart to Avalokiteshvara, the bodhisattva of compassion.

The drupchen and teachings were held at the Domaine de Lembrun retreat center about an hour north of Toulouse. I spent a few days in Toulouse before and after the retreat.

Orgyen Tobgyal Rinpoche and Neton Chokling Rinpoche were also in attendance. I had never met Chokling Rinpoche before. For me, this was a wonderful surprise. It completed my desire to be in the presence of all the prominent Rime teachers from the time of Jamyang Khyentse Wangpo, Chokgyur Lingpa, and Jamgön Kongtrul. I made a nice connection with Neton Chokling Rinpoche and we spent some time talking outside during some breaks. He has a very calm and gentle way of being.

Physically, the drupchen was difficult. There were many who had housing but I stayed in a tent on the encampment grounds. It rained many of the days, creating a slushy mud environment. Going to the porto-potties during the breaks was especially challenging. I didn't take notes during the daily talk given by Jigme Khyentse Rinpoche so I don't have much to share that I still

---

5   Personal notes from Jigme Khyentse Rinpoche teachings in Portugal, April 3-4, 2016.

Watercolor of White Tara by author, 2023.

remember. I do remember Rinpoche gave a wonderful talk on the three samadhis reminding us that we are the deity with all the retinue around. Visualization practice, recognizing oneself as the deity, purifies our perception of ourself as an ordinary person. He also gently chastised us regarding showing up late for the sadhana practice. With this, he skillfully drove us from our cocoons into more heartfelt participation in the drupchen.

Several mornings I crawled out of my cocoon mind and sleeping bag into the cold damp air half cursing the guru who is always right. I have never been that great enthusiast of the elaborate Tibetan rituals of puja with all the mantras, mudras, and music. Something shifted during the drupchen which seemed to open a door that gave me a glimpse into the nature of empowerment and puja.

The sadhana practice with its bells, horns, cymbals, drums, and mantras reverberating through the room seemed to make a connection to a pure realm of Arya Tara, creating a bridge for blessings to descend, transforming our dualistic samsaric mind into pure perception, or at least offering us a glimpse when we managed to just let go. Is this Nagarjuna's meaning when he says "There is no samsara distinct from nirvana, no nirvana distinct from samsara"?

If there is no true existence, this seeming reality is free and open to be the pure realm. Then you add the blessings of the guru to the mix, who is no different from the Buddha or Arya (Noble) Tara who channels the blessings of the lineage coming directly from the aspirations of enlightened beings in their pure realms. Yet somehow all this marvelous display, this manifestation of rigpa is empty, non-existent, endowed with clarity, awareness, compassion, and infused with the presence of Tara.

Jigme Khyentse Rinpoche during a drupchen, Southern France, May 2019.

During one break in the practice, I asked Rinpoche for his blessing. True to his style he asked what I wanted his blessing for. I said for the possibility of attaining enlightenment in this lifetime and helping sentient beings. This does sound like a very stock Buddhist answer, but it is what I ask for at least once a day during practice.

Tsoknyi Rinpoche

Tsoknyi Rinpoche, Kham, Tibet, 2005.

In 2000, I heard Tsoknyi Rinpoche would be teaching a Dzogchen retreat in Colorado. I applied to attend the retreat. I was informed that this advanced retreat was open only to students who had attended three of Rinpoche's previous retreats. This was very disappointing. I wrote a letter to Rinpoche expressing my desire to come to this Dzogchen retreat. In the email, I told him the dream I had of meeting him while I was on the flight to Nepal. Rinpoche granted permission for me to attend his teachings.

Tsoknyi Rinpoche has a different teaching approach than many of the Tibetan Rinpoches who teach Western students. In open retreats, he will give the pointing out instructions to novice Buddhists. I believe he follows the Dzogchen approach of his father Tulku Urgyen Rinpoche. This style is to point directly to the nature of the mind and then during the path or meditation practice one attempts to recognize this nature of mind, or rigpa and rest there. In an interview Tsoknyi Rinpoche gave at Wisdom

House in Litchfield, Connecticut he described his teaching style.

> My approach is first to communicate what is called the ground, the Buddha-nature, and then, when explaining what is called the path stage, its juice—the view—I try to bring the individual practitioner face to face with what is called the view of their own nature of mind. Once that has happened, there's some kind of insight that takes place in personal experience. That is what needs to be developed and deepened. So how to go about that? Only by focusing on that and nothing else? Or to use other methods, such as taking refuge, developing bodhicitta—the resolve to attain enlightenment for the benefit of all beings—accumulating merit, and so forth. These other practices deepen compassion and other important qualities. I feel that if one combines the insight into the nature of mind together with these other practices, they help you to progress much faster. Many people attending practiced Vipassana or Zen for twenty or more years, and when they come into contact with the Dzogchen teachings, their practice and the Dzogchen teachings are mutually beneficial. The Vipassana system is a very sound, steady way of progressing, and there's a model of slowly reaching some level of perfection. Conceptual habits begin to dissolve because of the training. The subject-object, conceptual attitude wears out, wears down, and fades away. But let's say that if, like two-thirds of the way on that path, that person came into contact with the Dzogchen teachings, then maybe just within the next year the same progress could be made that may otherwise have taken ten more years.[1]

As I mentioned earlier, my experience as a student of Trungpa Rinpoche was different. He presented a complete nine-yana

---

1 Personal notes from Tsoknyi Rinpoche teaching at Wisdom House in Litchfield, CT, circa 2003.

approach that delineated the Buddhist path in great detail. The Hinayana path, emphasizing formal meditation practice and mindfulness was where we began our journey. Trungpa Rinpoche used the metaphor of Hinayana being the strong foundation of a highrise without which the whole building (path) might collapse. There was then a natural progression into the Mahayana path and eventually to the fruition of Vajrayana, Mahamudra or Maha Ati from Dzogchen. Trungpa Rinpoche mostly taught Mahamudra, the ultimate teaching of the Kagyu path. Before receiving a Yidam empowerment and deity yoga sadhana practice we were required to complete the four preliminary practices, *ngöndro*. This involves 100,000 each of prostrations, Vajrasattva mantra, mandala offerings, and guru yoga. The pointing-out instructions came after this.

Although Tsoknyi Rinpoche's approach may on the surface differ from Trungpa Rinpoche's, there seems to be something about his direct style that reminds many of Trungpa Rinpoche. You will find many of Trungpa's former students at Tsoknyi Rinpoche's retreats.

Two or three days into the "advanced" retreat I felt lost and confused. I was listening to Rinpoche's teaching on Dzogchen with no background from his previous retreats. I felt like I had jumped into a raging river and didn't know how to swim. I realized why he and his organization, Pundarika, placed restrictions and requirements on these teachings. Someone at the retreat informed me that Tsoknyi Rinpoche only gave the pointing out instruction of the nature of mind at beginning retreats. The idea that I might go through the entire retreat without receiving the pointing-out instructions disturbed me.

On the second day of the retreat, I approached Tsoknyi Rinpoche who was sitting in his car after the teaching. I expressed my gratitude for his allowing me to attend the retreat. I said, "You might not realize this but I never received the pointing out instructions from you and I am feeling rather confused during your teachings." He said, "Don't worry, I will give it."

On the following day he gave the pointing out instructions. The moment Rinpoche gave the instruction all thoughts vanished and this mind, for a moment free from distraction, entered a quiet, empty, and luminous space. Tsoknyi Rinpoche looked like a

Buddha sitting on his throne and the shrine room seemed bathed in a golden radiance.

For the next few years, I spent a lot of time with Tsoknyi Rinpoche in Crestone Colorado where his sangha had built him a house and intended to build a center. I even purchased land in Crestone and spent a year building a home there. I intended to move there in the future but as it turned out I never did, and eventually I sold the house. One day, visiting Rinpoche in his home, he told me he would be going to Tibet on a pilgrimage to visit his nunneries and see his teacher Adeu Rinpoche. I asked if I could come along. He thought for a moment and then said, "I think you are low maintenance. You can come."

View of valley from Osel Ling Monastery, Kathmandu, Nepal, 2005.

In 2005, after traveling through northern India and Ladakh, Kathy and I spent a few weeks practicing in Rinpoche's monastery, Osel Ling, before our trip to Tibet. Osel Ling is located on the outskirts of Kathmandu with a spectacular view of the Kathmandu valley. It was founded by Tsoknyi Rinpoche's father, Tulku Urgyen Rinpoche and is now home to over 100 monks.

In late June, Tsoknyi Rinpoche led our small group of students, including a film crew, to visit his nuns and nunneries in Nangchen, Tibet (now part of China). Nangchen is in the southernmost part of the Qinghai Province of China. We arrived in Xinging, the capital of Qinghai, and the largest city of the Tibetan Plateau. We were met by Rinpoche's friend Tashi Galsten Rinpoche who organized all the details of our travels through Kham.

The next morning, Tosknyi Rinpoche explained the two principal reasons for our trip. He had come to receive teachings on the Six Yogas of Naropa from his teacher Adeu Rinpoche. He also wanted to document the lives and practice of the Nangchen Nuns. For this, we had Victress Hitchcock, an accomplished director, along with her film crew. I was there as a still photographer. The intention was to use both the documentary and the photographs to gather funds to help support the nuns.

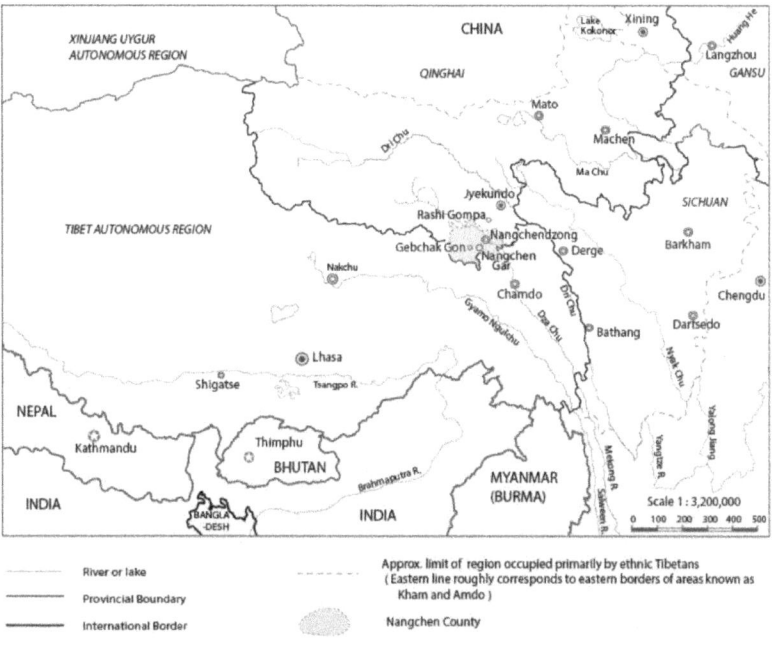

Map of Nangchen area, including Gebchak Monastery, Tibet.
Map courtesy of Jampa Kalden.

We left early the next morning before sunrise and loaded into five all-terrain vehicles. We traveled through Kham along the National Highway southwest towards Jyekundo. Along the way, we passed through grasslands and alpine forests of the Tibetan Plateau. We passed by Khampa nomads with their yaks and tent camps. At the top of a steep mountain pass marked with Tibetan prayer flags we made our first stop. Tsoknyi Rinpoche led us in tossing handfuls of paper windhorses into the sky. We shouted "Ki ki so so lha gyal lo." This is the warrior's cry that invokes the energy of windhorse.

It can be translated as "may the gods be victorious."

As our car stopped along the 5,500-meter-high road past Gangbala Mountain, the Tibetan farmers sitting beside us gave me a pile of wind horses—colored paper printed with Buddhist portraits and scriptures. All of sudden, our car drove out of the valley and a wide-open vista unfolded before us—white *kata* (long silk scarves), colored prayer flags, tall piles of *mani* (holy stone carvings) and a crystal clear lake. The car windows were all open and the Tibetan farmers threw the wind horses into air while chanting sorry to disturb you, mountain and water gods.

We headed to Yushu where Adeu Rinpoche's monastery was located. It was an arduous drive through creeks and over mountain passes. Arriving in Yushu we were greeted by a motorcade of cars and motorcycles. Rugged Khampa devotees lined up along the road waving white katas. Rinpoche stopped to offer the blessings they were seeking. All along the journey, we encountered Khampa nomads waiting with their katas. In this vast isolated land without internet and few telephones, I do not how the Tibetans always knew when and where Rinpoche would be passing by but somehow they did. It was the custom to always greet us outside the village. After the blessings, we were then escorted to the town center.

Khampa devotees greet us in Yushu, Tibet, 2005.

The next day, July 25th, 2005 we went to the annual Yushu Horse Festival. Nomads from across the region of Kham had set up tents for the weeklong festival. The Khampa men and women were dressed in their finest long-sleeve chubas. There were traditional dances, picnic feasts of yak yogurt, momos, and blood sausages. There was folk singing and dancing. Then the horse racing began.

Yushu Horse Festival, Tibet, 2005.

From Yushu, we traveled to Sharda, the ancient capital of the Kingdom of Nangchen. The King of Nangchen and large numbers of Khampa nomads lined the road, ready to receive Rinpoche. Modern-day motorcycle Khampa cowboys offered bouquets of flowers with multi-colored ribbons.

Khampa men on motorcycles coming to greet Tsoknyi Rinpoche, Nangchen, Tibet, 2005.

We next visited Tari Gong, Tashi Gyeltsen Rinpoche's monastery, and visited the old hermitage of Pe Chor Gyor, a disciple of the first Tsokyi Rinpoche. We were shown a large rock embedded in the mountainside where there were footprints of this great yogi. In my travels in India and Nepal I have had footprints of Padmasambhava and other yogis pointed out to me but these were the clearest and most believable I had seen, showing clearly the stride of someone walking.

Yogi footprints in the rock, somewhere in Nangchen, Tibet.

This was our first time meeting with the Nangchen Nuns. A small group of young nuns came out of their three-year retreat to meet Tsoknyi Rinpoche and his students. The next night we arrived at Demo Gong, the seat of Tashi Gyalten's father Sangye Tagpa. A group of nuns greeted us by blowing long ganlang trumpets.

Entering a small dark room with Tsoknyi Rinpoche we greeted the yogi Rigsing Gyalchon. He told us a bit of his life story. After meeting the first Tsoknyi Rinpoche at the age of eight he began practicing Buddhadharma. He was now eighty. Being in the presence of Tsoknyi Rinpoche he said there were no teachings he could offer us. He did advise us to practice without distraction and then offered his blessings.

From there we traveled through the countryside crossing rivers over fragile dilapidated wooden bridges, driving on dirt roads and sometimes on no roads at all. Eventually, we came to an encampment where several local nuns, a small Khampa group, and

Nuns from Demo Gong, Nangchen, Tibet, playing ganlang trumpets, come to greet Tsoknyi Rinpoche, 2005.

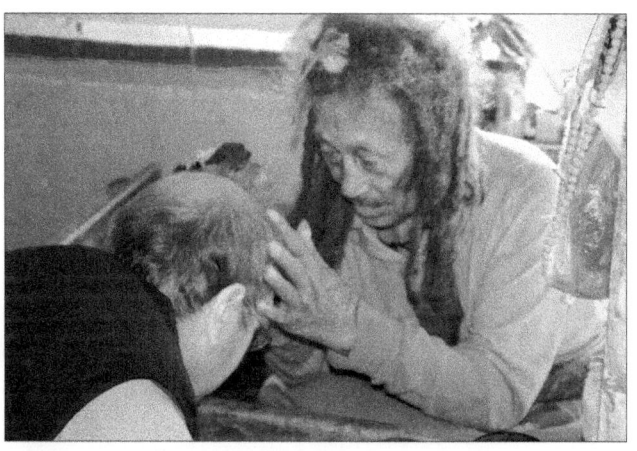

Author receiving blessing from Rigsing Gyalchon, Demo Gong, Kingdom of Nanchen, Tibet, 2005.

a Dechenling nun, were waiting for us. Khampa men, women, and children were helping everyone for the journey. They outfitted us with horses and led us for another six hours or more across the high mountains of the Tibetan Plateau.

Just before sunset, we arrived at Dechen Ling to the sound of Tibetan horns and cymbals. The nuns, dressed in their finest dakini robes, came out of a three-year retreat to greet their teacher.

The first Tsoknyi Rinpoche lived in Nangchen during the 19th century. The region is known as gomde, "the land of great

Pith Instructions from my Teachers

Nuns dressed in their finest dakini robes, Nangchen, Tibet, 2005.

meditators." He was a lineage holder of both the Drukpa Kagyu and Nyingma lineages and known for his mastery of the Six Yogas of Naropa. With the aspiration to create the same opportunities for women to practice as men, he instructed his closest disciple, Tsang Yang Gyamtso, to build a series of nunneries. Tsoknyi Rinpoche is the root guru of the Nangchen Nuns. He is a emanation of the terton Ratna Lingpa who taught the Heart Accomplishment of Guru Rinpoche and many other sadhanas that are practiced by the Nangchen Nuns.

Nangchen nuns with Khampa women meeting us with horses to go to Dechen Ling Nunnery, Nangchen, Tibet, 2005.

The landscape of Dechen Ling could have come straight from the movie *Lost Horizon* (1937) about the mythical Shangri La. The nuns live in individual earthen huts nestled against the mountainside. It felt like we had traveled into the past arriving at a place that existed in another century.

Dechen Ling, Nangchen, Tibet, 2005.

Tsoknyi Rinpoche III has characterized the heart of the practice of the Nangchen nuns as devotion and pure perception. Many nuns do three-year retreats, and nine-year retreats, and some remain in lifelong retreats. Nuns on retreat will practice day and night sitting in a three foot square wooden box only large enough to sit cross-legged. There is no room to lie down to sleep. Their typical day begins at 3:30 in the morning and will include four three-hour meditation sessions. They will continue practicing dream yoga throughout the night. Even though the Gebchak nuns are part of the Drukpa Kagyu lineage much of their practice follows the revealed treasure teaching of Ratna Lingpa. Gebchak is also famous for the practice of Tummo or inner heat.

One day Tsoknyi Rinpoche took us to see Mingyur Yogini, who was in a life-long retreat. She is one of the last living disciples of Tulku Urgyen Rinpoche's father Chimey Dorje and is considered a very realized nun. We climbed the hill to her retreat cave. When we arrived, Rinpoche directed us into her retreat cave where she was practicing in the traditional meditation box. With a smile that emanated peace and confidence, she gave us small

Pith Instructions from my Teachers

Tsoknyi Rinpoche, Mingyur yogini, and author (far left) with group that traveled through Nangchen, Tibet, 2005.

plastic bags of *dutsi* (blessing substance). At the urging of Tsoknyi Rinpoche, she came out of her retreat cave.

As far as I have discovered, the nunnery was destroyed when the Chinese invaded and the nuns went and hid in the mountains. After some years, they came out of hiding and the nunnery was rebuilt.

After Dechenling, we returned by horseback to where we had left the jeeps and then continued on to Gebchak, considered the mother monastery.

Gebchak consists of a large central Abbey and several small earthen huts where up to a dozen nuns will live and practice together. The nuns of Gebchak are known for their mastery of the practice of *tummo* (inner heat). In Tulku Urgyen Rinpoche's memoirs, *Blazing Splendor*, he recalls the inner heat (*tummo*) practice of the Getchak nuns. In the middle of the Tibetan winter, hundreds of nuns show their mastery of the practice called the wet sheet. Beginning at midnight they dip sheets in buckets of snow-melted water and wrap their naked bodies in the wet sheets. Tulku Urgyen describes seeing the misty vapors evaporating as the sheets dry from their body heat from a long line of nuns walking in eight directions around the monastery.

The conditions the nuns live in are very harsh by Western stan-

Mingyur yogini, Nangchen, Tibet, 2005.

dards. Most of the time we slept in cold rooms, often with just our pads on the floor. The food consisted of *tsampa* (ground barley flour mixed with salty butter tea) and a leafy green similar to mustard greens. Sometimes there was yak or actually *dri* (female yak) yogurt, a yak cheese shaped into tiny rock-hard peas or dried yak meat that tasted more like cardboard than meat. If you didn't want a colored Chinese soda the option was dri butter tea, for which I had not developed a taste.

The latrines were gaps between planks of wood secured on the mountainsides enclosed by plastic sheeting. I often thought about how hard the lives of these nuns were and what a spoiled American I was, so attached to all my comforts—central heating,

Pith Instructions from my Teachers

Three nuns from Gebchak monastery, Nangchen, Tibet, 2005.

a hot shower, fresh fruits and vegetables, a pharmacy. I watched nuns lugging heavy jugs of water up the hill to the monastery on a cold morning. Others were on the hillside herding Yaks. Often, they were singing or chanting mantras. There were no complaints.

The nearest medical clinics to most monasteries were more than a day's drive, two or more days on horseback. The shortage of water for cleaning and bathing along with the general lack of understanding of basic hygiene lead to infections and other illnesses. I heard that one in four women in Kham dies during childbirth due to unsanitary conditions. Avoiding pregnancy is one of the motivations for becoming a nun.

In spite of the harshness of their surroundings, the nuns always appeared happy and content. An inner wealth radiated from their faces. The effects of the life of Buddhist practice could not be denied.

The nuns did all the work to maintain monastic life. At all the nunneries I never saw monks work to clean or cook. I witnessed the nuns obtaining all the food. One day I watched a man riding up with a yak carcass strapped to the horse he led. A group of nuns went to greet him. He yanked the yak's body off the horse.

The nuns with large knives began chopping up the meat.

During pujas the monks sat closer to the front where Rinpoches conducted the ceremony. The seating order of events was the monks sat in front, then the nuns and the locals and foreigners sat against the back wall. This is typical of monastic hierarchy.

Pema Trimey at his retreat center in Nangchen, Tibet, 2005.

After several days at Gebchak we rode on horseback to Pema Trimey's retreat center. Pema Trimey is an advanced yogi who leads *Tögal* or 'leaping over' retreats. We were fortunate to have the opportunity of interviewing him in a small room with Tsoknyi Rinpoche translating. This was his first teaching to Westerners. He stressed the importance of realizing the nature of mind. He was willing to answer any questions related to *trechö* or *tögal*. I asked him about the togal experience of vajra chains or *dorje lugu gyü*. This was an experience along the togal path I remembered Trungpa Rinpoche once talking about. Usually, these were considered hidden teachings. After a short stay and blessing by Pema Trimey, we returned to Gebchak Gonpa.

The next day, half of us accompanied Tsoknyi Rinpoche to Dzongo Ling (Fortress Peak), the hermitage of Samten Gyaltso and later Tsoknyi Rinpoche's father Tulku Urgyen Rinpoche. Fortress Peak is one of the most magnificent places I have ever vis-

Dzongo Ling (Fortress Peak) Retreat Center, Nangchen, Tibet, 2005.

ited. The retreat center and stupa sit in a valley surrounded by mountains on all sides. The site has been used by Buddhists for thousands of years, including the early Tibetan practitioners of the Bon tradition. According to Erik Pema Kusang, "This mountain is regarded as the most sacred in the whole of the Nangchen kingdom—it is both the mandala of the peaceful and wrathful deities as well as that of Chakrasamvara."[2]

There is a small path, a hill behind the main building that leads up to a three-year retreat center and offers a great view of the surrounding mountains. On the lower level, there is a stupa atop a mound strewn with prayer flags.

After lunch, we had time to wander the hillside and enjoy the incredible views from Dzongo Ling. I don't think I have ever been to such a magical place. It was easy to understand why Tulku Urgyen Rinpoche, before being forced to leave Tibet, wanted to spend his life in retreat here.

The next morning, we headed back to Gebchak. During our stay, we were invited to meet Sherab Zangmo, who was considered the most realized nun in Gebchak and perhaps in all of Nangchen.

---

2   Erik Pema Kunsang. "Fortress Peak, the Cover Picture." *Blazing-Splendor* (blog), August 11, 2005. http://blazing-splendor.blogspot.com/2005/08/fortress-peak-cover-picture.html.

Dzongo Ling (Fortress Peak), Nangchen, Tibet, 2005.

We crowded into the small dark room and sat shoulder to shoulder. Black stalactites covered the ceiling from the years of soot created by the wood burning stove. My eyes teared from the fumes of incense and the yak dung smoke leaking from the crude wood stove. In the dark corner, light spilled from the doorway illuminating an ancient face, her deep wrinkles etched from the harsh Tibetan life at 14,000 feet. There, leaning back in her meditation box was Sherab Zangmo spinning her prayer wheel.

When Sherab Zangmo was a young nun, during a dark retreat (a Dzogchen practice of staying in total darkness for 49 days and nights), she had a vision of Yeshe Tsogyal, Guru Rinpoche's principal consort. She described her experience to us.

> Three times she offered me mudras (hand gestures) and then she became Tsang Yang Gyamtso (the student of the first Tsoknyi Rinpoche who started Getchak Nunnery). He came to rest on top of my head and then he dissolved into my body, speech, and mind. We became one. I cried and cried. At that moment I had a direct experience of the nature of my

mind. I have had many experiences, good and bad, but my mind has remained stable, neither good nor bad.³

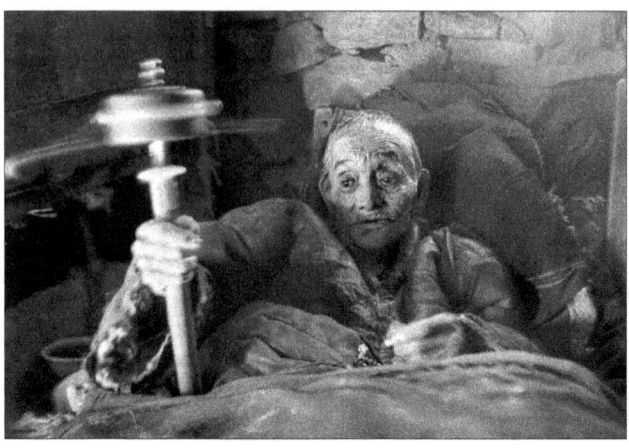

Sherab Zangmo, Gebchak Nunnery, Tibet, 2005.

I asked Sherab Zangmo if she could describe her perception of the world. She replied, "What arises in my mind now is the thought to benefit others. On the other hand, I don't cling to appearances as real, in the way that others do.

Wangdrag Rinpoche, the head of Gebchak nunnery, asked her, "Do they appear like a dream?"

"Yes, they appear illusory, like a dream," she said.

When we left Sherab Zangmo her prayer wheel was spinning and she was reciting the Vajrasattva hundred-syllable mantra. Sherab Zangmo died a year later. The nuns reported that her heart stayed warm for several days after her death. The Tibetans call this tukdam which sometimes occurs after the death of highly realized beings.

On August 14th we left Gebchak Gonpa to meet the yogi and meditation master Pema Dorje in his remote hermitage in Mokphur. Pema Dorje was revered by all the Gebchak nuns. It is said that after many years of solitary practice at his isolated mountain hermitage he became locally known for his yogic practice. He had developed the siddhi or capability for preventing thunder-

---

3   Zangmo, Sherab. Interview by James Gritz, 2005.

storms, helping to guard the fields and harvest of the rural people living around Wakha village. We were told that one of his own teachers had been a Gebchak nun. Although he had spent the majority of his life in strict retreat, he was a teacher to most of the older Gebchak nuns.

He appeared like a crazy yogi with his hair tied back in long dreadlocks. He walked around the hermitage singing and shouting Tibetan syllables. He reminded me of Ponlop Rinpoche's root teacher Khenpo Tsultrim Gyamtso Rinpoche. Yogi Pema Dorje died in January 2014 with all the signs of a highly realized master.

Pema Dorje in his remote hermitage in Mokphur, Tibet, 2005.

At this point in our journey the group divided. A few of us returned with Tsoknyi Rinpoche to Gebchak where he would begin a Vajrayogini retreat in preparation for receiving the Six Yogas of Naropa. The filmmakers and the rest of the group went back to Jekyundo. From there they returned by way of Beijing where they all stayed in a five-star Hilton, recovering from the 'deprivation' they suffered in Tibet. When I finally left Tibet five months later, I would indulge myself in the same manner.

I remained in Nangchen at Gebchak with Rinpoche and a young western monk named Josh. I then decided to go into retreat. The nuns set up a tent on the hill below where Tsoknyi Rinpoche was doing his retreat. Every day a young nun brought me food, water, and tea, making it possible for me to remain in retreat without any need to come down to the monastery.

Tsoknyi Rinpoche encourages retreats, especially for students who have spent some time practicing Dharma.

> If you really want to progress on the path, you have to do retreat. We have to put effort into our practice because we have a long history of grasping onto hope and fear and creating karmic debts. So, it is very important to create periods of time to focus exclusively on practice and break these old habits. If we only meditate for short periods of time, progress can be a little bit difficult. In retreat, you're looking in rather than looking out. When you're not in retreat you're looking outside and engaging in a lot of external activities and problems. But in retreat, your mind's attention is looking in, so whatever you have in your files, whatever you have stored in your database, starts to come up. At this point, it may feel that you have more anger, more attachment because now it's coming into awareness. When this starts to happen, what you should do is see how you can just let it go.[4]

Because I am restless and impatient by nature, I find the first few days of retreat trying. To sit with your own mind without the distraction of your usual diversions brings on an irritating boredom. Even after all my years on the path I still was not good at accepting what Trungpa Rinpoche called cool boredom. Between practice sessions I went for short walks. One day, driven by restlessness and curiosity, I went up the hill to where Tsoknyi Rinpoche was in retreat in a small house the monks and nuns had built for him. Hearing him reciting a Vajrayogini mantra I was encouraged to

---

4   Tsoknyi Rinpoche. "Rinpoche Discusses Retreat." Pundarika Foundation, June 26, 2017. https://tsoknyirinpoche.org/yeshe-rangsal/places-to-practice-2/an-interview-concerning-retreat-with-tsoknyi-rinpoche/

return to my tent to practice more diligently. After a few days my mind slowed down and my practice became more spacious. When I wasn't doing my sadhana and visualization practice I would just sit, gazing out into the vast open landscape. Sometimes, on clear days I would do a sky gazing practice Rinpoche had taught during several retreats in Colorado or watch the yak on the hillside.

The view down the hillside from my tent of Samtem Gyaltsen house at Gebchak.

When I left retreat, Josh and I decided to make our way to Nangchen Gar while Tsoknyi Rinpoche was still in retreat. Nangchen Gar, also known as Tsechu Monastery, was the home of Tsoknyi Rinpoche's teacher Adeu Rinpoche. Tsoknyi Rinpoche told me that when the Chinese invaded Tibet in 1950, Adeu Rinpoche was captured and sent to a prison camp in Xining, one of the worst in Tibet. It was specially designed for khenpos and incarnate lamas. Although he was imprisoned for 15 years, his patience and compassion never faded.

He stated that his years in prison were, in fact, an extraordinary opportunity to practice. It also gave him the opportunity to

Pith Instructions from my Teachers

Nangchen Gar Monastery, Nangchen, Tibet, 2005.

meet a number of great masters who were also imprisoned. He received Dzogchen and other Nyingma treasure teachings. Because so many Drukpa Kagyu masters were killed during the Cultural Revolution, Adeu Rinpoche was the last lineage holder of the complete Drugpa Kagyu teachings. These he passed on to Tsoknyi Rinpoche and other tulkus. Tsoknyi Rinpoche is a lineage holder but Adeu Rinpoche was the last to have all the teachings. Many he passed on to Tsoknyi Rinpoche. In fact when I was there Tsoknyi Rinpoche asked me to film Adeu Rinpoche performing a special Drugpa Kagyu Vajrayogini practice so that this could be passed on to other Drugpa Kagyu monasteries.

After his release from Chinese prison, Adeu Rinpoche worked on rebuilding Tsechu Gonpa, which had been nearly totally destroyed by the Chinese. Adeu Rinpoche was a master of the six yogas of Naropa and held the complete treasure teachings of Ratna Lingpa. Tsoknyi Rinpoche is considered an emanation of Ratna Lingpa. The relationship between the Tsoknyi and Adeu Rinpoche incarnations had always been extremely close with the two alternating between student and teacher in different lifetimes.

I ended up spending five months with Tsoknyi Rinpoche at Nangchen Gar while Rinpoche, along with yogis from all over Tibet, received the teachings of the Six Yogas of Naropa from Adeu Rinpoche. The Six Yogas are one of the most advanced completion stage yogic practices in the Tibetan Buddhist Kagyu tradition. It is

Adeu Rinpoche at Nangchen Gar, 2005.

said that they contain the essential and complete tantric practices necessary for attaining enlightenment in one lifetime. They were compiled by the *mahasiddha* Naropa from various original tantras. Including *tummo* or inner heat practice they form the basis for the inner yoga practices of Mahamudra.

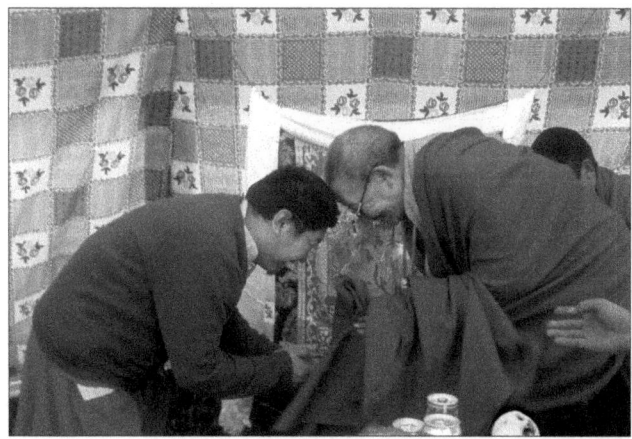

Adeu Rinpoche and Tsoknyi Rinpoche at Nangchen Gar, 2005.

Pith Instructions from my Teachers

My yogi neighbor during my stay at Nangchen Gar, 2005.

I had hoped to partake in the Six Yogas of Naropa teachings. Close to the end of our stay at Gebchak, Tsoknyi Rinpoche warned me I could not attend the teachings on the six yogas. He said the teachings would be long and rigorous and everything would be in Tibetan. He told me he was receiving these teachings for the first time himself and he would not have the time to translate for me. Probably seeing my disappointment, Rinpoche then said he would give me any other teachings I wanted to receive but I would not be able to attend these teachings.

I ended up sharing a small room at Nangchen Gar with Josh, the western monk from New York. A few weeks later Brady, Rinpoche's secretary, joined us. We all passed the time doing our personal practices in our room or walking around the countryside nestled in the mountains of Tsechu.

Many Western students of Tibetan Buddhism have a romantic fantasy that going to Tibet is a great way to do retreat and practice. In my opinion it is much easier to do retreat in your home or in a quiet mountain cabin near where you live. We were three in a small room. Next door to us was a yogi with a nun attending him who slept on the floor in the corner of his room. Down the hall was a bathroom where you could squat and shit between two boards. It was cold in the morning and evenings. There was a very small wood stove in the yogi's room next door but nothing in ours. Mostly we practiced wrapped in our sleeping bags. There was no such thing as privacy. Monks or nuns walk through the door unannounced without knocking. I think knocking on a door is a western custom and so is complaining about your conditions.

Nangchen Gar or Tsechu Gonpa is a Drukpa Kagyu monastery two hours by taxi from the town of Sechu. In the 19th century, the terton Chokgyur Lingpa grew up as a monk under the care of one of the previous incarnations of Adeu Rinpoche. The previous Adeu Rinpoche was also one of Chökgyur Lingpa's teachers. Adeu Rinpoche said, "There is a particular guidance manual in Dzogchen which was requested by Chökgyur Lingpa and written by the previous Adeu Rinpoche called *The Oral Teachings of Vajrasattva*. Chökgyur Lingpa had transmitted this to his son Tsewang Norbu, who gave it to Samten Gyatso and then he passed it on to me again."[5]

Samten Gyatso was one of the grandsons of Chökgyur Lingpa. Erik Pema Kunsang explains his relationship to the *Chokling Tersar*, a cycle of teaching all my teachers hold. "It is thanks to Samten Gyatso that the *Chokling Tersar* was spread far and wide because neither Tsikey Chokling nor Uncle Tersey ever transmitted it in full. Of that generation, only Neten Chokling did so, but only once. That is why Tsewang Norbu pointed them out at Riwoche."Basically, the transmission of the *Chokling Tersar* that all the great lamas of those days received came through Samten Gyatso. He gave the *Chokling Tersar* three times in Central Tibet.

Many great lamas received the transmission then, including the omniscient 15th Karmapa, the great Drukchen, Taklung Tsetrul, and the three masters with the title Jamgön who resided at Jang Taklung. The cycles of teachings of Chögyur Lingpa make up some of my main practices that I have received from Tsoknyi

---

5 Erik Solomo. "Interview with Adeu Rinpoche for Chokling Tersar Times." *Erik Pema Kunsang Among Masters: A Live Biography*, October 3, 1999. http://erik-pema-kunsang-a-live-biography.blogspot.com/p/blog-page_3367.html

Rinpoche, Dzongsar Khyentse, and Ponlop Rinpoche. This is not surprising, since Chökgyur Lingpa was one of the three great Rime teachers. He also once lived at Nangchen Gar, Adeu Rinpoche's monastery but left because he had a fight or didn't like the King of Nangchen who lived there or nearby. These stories help me to contextualize my teachers and their teachings.

One day I was sitting with Adeu and Tsoknyi Rinpoches at his nunnery a couple hours on foot from the monastery. The three of us were crammed on a small wooden platform outside Adeu Rinpoche's room. It was a great place to meditate with an inspiring panoramic view. Adeu Rinpoche pointed to a mountain across the valley and said that is where Chogyur Lingpa discovered one of Guru Rinpoche's treasures.

I found my stay in Tibet both inspiring and arduous. Three of us practiced in a small room with nuns often passing by to see what we were doing. Of course, the mountains and valleys are beautiful and there were plenty of places to sit and practice. I often craved a decent meal, a good bed, and a hot shower. I think I turned out not to be the low-maintenance person Tsoknyi Rinpoche thought I was. One day, tired of the lack of privacy in our room, I approached Tsoknyi Rinpoche as he was coming downstairs from his quarters. I asked him if there was someplace where I could go and practice in a room of my own where I would not be bothered. I started to

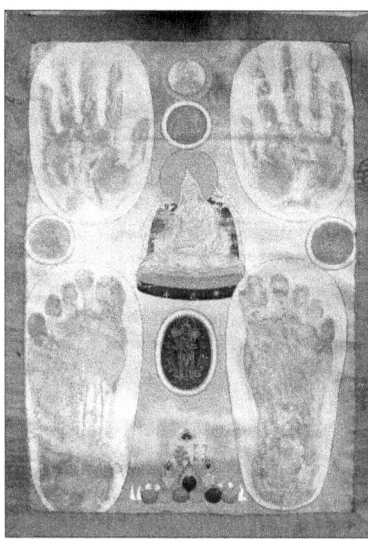

L > Chogyur Lingpa
M > Jamyang Khyentse Wango
R > Jamgon Kongtrul

These 3 thangkas were displayed at a teaching by Dzongsar Jamyang Khyentse Rinpoche in Vancouver, 2013.

explain the situation but he interrupted and said: "just deal with it!" In a way this was a pith instruction. I felt I truly lacked renunciation. Many times, I have heard that one should bring suffering onto the path and be willing to deal with it. In a later retreat in Germany, Tsoknyi Rinpoche said there is a Tibetan saying: "throw your food, clothing and fame, toss it to the wind." He said for retreat, just bring what you need to survive and concentrate on your practice. I went back to my room.

I cooked for Rinpoche often with or without his long-time attendant. On occasion, I made the drive by taxi to Sechu to buy supplies and food. This was a great break that enabled me to have lunch and a hot shower at the local bathhouse. I realized during my stay that I was not much of a yogi. I'm sure the real yogis who came from all over Tibet viewed their stay at Nangchen Gar as a kind of vacation.

Several months into my stay at Nangchen Gar my friend Tashi Gyaltsen Rinpoche came to the monastery. He invited me to come with him to visit a school he had started in Nangchen and a small nunnery he was responsible for. On the way, after climbing one mountain pass, we stopped to pay our respects to a sacred waterfall. The water was said to come directly from Tara, the female deity associated with compassion and enlightened activity, protecting beings from fear.

There was a narrow creek to cross before getting to the waterfall. I was carrying an expensive video camera I had purchased from my friend Josh. Feeling confident, I decided to jump to a rock in the middle of the creek to get to the other side. Although it looked sound it turned out the rock was slimy and holding the camera up with my right hand I slipped into the creek. My elbow smashed into a rock and my body completely submerged into the water. I am not sure if Tara was mad at me or blessing me with the water, but there at 15,000 feet I was drenched on my coldest day in Tibet.

I didn't have a change of clothes but fortunately one of the women in our jeep had a blanket. As the night was falling it began to snow. We were driving across open country without roads. One of the jeeps slid down the hill. I was too wet to go out into the freezing snow. Everyone tried to push the jeep up the hill but it was too steep. I waited, shivering in the car, thinking this might be the night I died in the first snowstorm of the year. In the distance we saw lights approaching. A large group of nomads came out of nowhere with ropes to help pull out the jeep.

When we arrived at the school, I huddled in the kitchen with the two western women who were traveling with us. The Chinese drivers were nervous we would get stuck here in this snowstorm. The next day we made it to the nunnery. It was almost all destroyed. The nuns only had a few rooms left to live in. I don't

Nangchen Nuns in first snowstorm of 2005.

know the whole story, but I was told that after Tsoknyi Rinpoche gave the nunnery to Tashi Gyeltson, its rightful and historic heir, a rival Rinpoche who considered this nunnery his property came with a truck full of monks and with sledgehammers destroyed the nunnery.

My friend Brady Hogan, at the time Tsoknyi Rinpoche's secretary, wrote this in her travelog:

> This place beats all for the most challenging place that I have ever spent time, with the lack of heat, running water, electric, phone. The most basic comforts are non-existent. It is not just the lack of these, but rather the exposure, the vastness, the bareness, the unforgiving intensity of the elements at play with the lack of protection that challenges the psyche. There is no place to hide.[6]

I whole heartedly agree, and Brady is a hard-core woman used to living in Nepal and Asia. As a photographer I have traveled throughout the world to capture images, many times to remote places like Borneo, Africa, India, Cambodia, and Nepal, but for me Tibet was the most arduous country to spend an extended time. To feel at ease you have to come out of your cocoon and give up all the comforts to which you are accustomed. For me the lack of tasty food and clean places to remove it were most trying. In general, we westerners are very spoiled.

After about five months, Rinpoche's wife Chimela came and stayed for a while. She planned to return to Kathmandu with Tashi Gyeltsan Rinpoche and stop to visit her mother in Lhasa. I told Rinpoche that I felt there was not much point in me continuing longer in Tibet. He was busy with Adeu Rinpoche's teachings and giving audiences and blessings to those who came from great distances to see him. There was also something competitive going on with his attendant and he much preferred to prepare Rinpoche's food without me. I asked Rinpoche if I could return to Nepal with Chimila and Tashi Gyeltsan Rinpoche. He said sure, you have been here 5 months, that's good enough. I later regretted that decision

---

6   Brady Hogan, personal travelogue shared with James Gritz, 2005.

as it would be the last time I would see Adeu Rinpoche. I asked Rinpoche if we could do a Vajrasattva feast from the sadhana I was practicing before I left. A monk found the text in Tibetan and with a couple of other monks we practiced the Tsok together.

After Rinpoche returned from Tibet I attended his first retreat in Mexico. I didn't realize at the time that Mexico would later become my home. The retreat was sponsored by Casa Tibet and held in a center near Tenancingo. For years that followed, I continued to attend Tsoknyi Rinpoche's month-long practice retreats in Crestone Colorado. In these retreats, three sessions of daily practice are mixed with two Dharma talks a day. All of Rinpoche's retreats are held in silence. I find this style of retreat, which eliminates discursive encounters, very helpful in developing a deeper experiential understanding of meditation practice.

One particular month-long retreat that took place in Crestone in August of 2009 stands out in my mind. During the first week Rinpoche gave three empowerments from the *Chokling Tersar* cycle of teachings—a Guru Rinpoche, Vajrasattva and Tara. He told the retreatants that if they wanted to start a deity yoga practice, they could choose whatever yidam they felt most connected to. Since I had already received the same Vajrasattva empowerment from Ponlop Rinpoche and that was my daily practice I had no decision to make.

For the next three weeks we moved from the Crestone College to a Tibetan tent on Pundarika land where Rinpoche taught on Gampopa's *The Precious Garland of the Sublime Path.*[7] This text includes lots of 10 things to do and not to do on the path. There were 10 useless things, 10 ways to destroy yourself, 10 necessities, etc. This was a big change from Tsoknyi Rinpoche's usual Dzogchen teachings. The teachings presented a practical guide to the three Yana path. Outside of the three hours of daily teaching in the big tent, we practiced another seven hours divided into three sessions in whatever locations we were staying. I find this kind of retreat, based on the Tibetan yogi camp style of daily teaching and isolated personal practice, the perfect way to assimilate the Dharma.

---

7 For further reading, I suggest this commentary on the teachings of Gampopa by Khenpo Karthar Rinpoche. *The Instructions of Gampopa: A Precious Garland of the Supreme Path (Dream Flag Series)*. Translated by Lama Yeshe Gyamtso. Ithaca, NY: Snow Lion Publications, 1996.

The underlying theme of the retreat seemed to be summarized by this quote from the Buddha that we found one morning on our zafus: "My dream-like form appears to dream-like beings to show the dream-like path to dream-like enlightenment." For me the entire retreat was like a waking dream. Toward the end of the retreat Rinpoche called for more audience participation to share either our own personal experiences or words of wisdom we had learned. Here are two of my favorite quotes:

> "Since everything is but an apparition, having nothing to do with good or bad, acceptance or rejection, one may as well burst out in laughter"—*Longchenpa*

> "If you don't know it's a thought it becomes your reality."—*Unknown*

During the retreat, I had one epiphany that was not a dream or *nyam*. I was practicing in my tent where I was camped by a river on a friend's land. It was late afternoon when I saw a sudden movement out the corner of my eye and heard a thump by the tree about ten feet away. My first thought was that the thump was way too big and loud to be a squirrel. Looking to my left I saw a mountain lion approaching my tent. My heart started beating rapidly. I keep chanting the Vajrasattva mantra. The lion walked past the large triangular screen window on the left of my shrine, about five feet from where I sat. It continued past the next screen window on the right. I was too scared to move and tried to keep my breath slow and soft. The thought arose that his giant paw could tear through the screen with one swipe. I thought it would be hard to rest naturally while being eaten. The lion continued walking past the tent without once looking in my direction.

I have photographed a lot of wildlife over the years—bears in Alaska, many animals in Africa, Borneo and Belize, even hammerhead sharks in the Galapagos, but this was really the closest I had ever been to a deadly predator. I finished an hour more practice, not because I was a great practitioner but because I was too scared to leave the tent. I wanted to give the lion plenty of time to wander away. I started to worry about the meaning of this experience. What are the odds of having a mountain lion approach when doing your sadhana practice in retreat. I ended the session with a lot of loud bell ringing and damaru drum playing.

I decided to go to the retreat tent to see if Tsoknyi Rinpoche was still there. As I was walking up the road, he was driving down from his group interview. He rolled down his window and asked me what's up. I told him about the encounter with the lion. He asked if I had food in my tent. Still shaken from the experience I had no clever retort and just said no. I said, "you think I should go back to the tent." He said, "Yes."

Geraldo, his translator, asked me how big the lion was. Rinpoche rolled up his window and they drove off. So matter of fact. I wasn't sure if Tsoknyi Rinpoche had some kind of clairvoyance or simply had no idea how dangerous a mountain lion was. I thought they probably didn't have mountain lions in Nepal.

I called my wife Kathy that night and she gave me some practical advice. She said, "Remember the movie *The Gods Must Be Crazy*? You should carry a big stick, make yourself look big, and walk with 360-degree awareness." So, for the next week I carried a long pole and said a lot of "om ah hums" and "phets" out loud as I walked down the path to my tent to make sure that if that lion was still around, he knew I was coming. I got a stiff neck from looking back so much but after a while the goose bumps went away. The lion never returned, or at least I never saw him again.

In 2011, I was in Bodhgaya filming and directing the documentary *Never Give Up* (2011). I was sitting one day with Tsoknyi Rinpoche in his room above the shrine hall at Tergar Monastery. He seemed very at ease, almost on vacation, the essence of carefree dignity. He told me he wanted to be working on his own devotion, working on developing his own bodhicitta, spending his time around the stupa making offerings.

Rinpoche once said:

> People may object to the idea of making offerings to the Buddha, Dharma and Sangha saying that you should instead give alms to the poor and needy—that is more useful. If we are only talking from the materialistic point of view, then this would be true. However, the Three Jewels, the precious Buddha, Dharma and Sangha are endowed with blessings.

In order to receive the blessings that are naturally present one needs to open up and totally let go of all levels of attachment in body, speech and mind. The way to do this is to relinquish clinging.

By the act of offering everything on an outer, inner and secret level we ensure that everything we could possibly cling to is relinquished. By opening up totally and letting go of all objects of clinging we become open to the blessings that naturally enter due to the power of former aspirations and vows of the Buddhas and Bodhisattvas.

It is not that the Buddhas and Bodhisattvas have any need for our offerings. In Tibet, some say they waste so much butter making butterlamps. How could the Buddhas and Bodhisattvas have any need for that? The fact is they don't. What happens while making an offering, for example lighting a butterlamp, is that one calls to mind the Buddhas and Bodhisattvas with a lot of appreciation. With great respect we call to mind the superior qualities of the Buddha's body, speech and mind, his virtues, activities and so forth and each time we bring these qualities to mind it changes us in some way. There is an instant of admiration that immediately takes place and it opens our minds.

When we light a butterlamp, we imagine not just this one lamp but innumerable lamps we are offering and we make the wish that these lamps will help dispel the darkness and ignorance of all sentient beings. All of these together—the devotion, keeping the qualities of enlightenment in mind, letting go of attachment, making offerings and the strong aspiration to benefit beings, coincide to perfect the accumulation of merit. So, it is much more than simply lighting a butterlamp.[8]

---

8   Personal notes from teaching by Tsoknyi Rinpoche, Gomde Retreat Center, Legget, CA, 1999.

It may have been Rinpoche's wish to spend his time circumambulating the Stupa but from the little I saw, developing his own bodhicitta seemed to take a different form. His mornings were filled with a constant flow of new and old students who came for advice, teachings, and blessings.

During an interview for our film *Never Give Up*, Tsoknyi Rinpoche told us this story.

> Bodhgaya is very special to me. So many things happen here due to the Buddha's blessings. Five years ago, here in Bodhgaya I thought I needed to change something. I looked into all my Buddhist practices. What do I need to improve? What do I need to change? I realized that I needed to improve Bodhicitta. I think of the comfortable Dharma practice I have. I usually call this California Dharma, where you make yourself feel very comfortable, cozy, mindful, relaxed, aware, love, love to others. All this makes you happy. If there is stress, the environment is not so good then I think OK, this is impermanent. You practice and visualize, Oh, this is a Buddha room. So, I make it very happy, cozy, joyful around myself in the name of Dharma.
>
> Real compassion is not being afraid to suffer for others. If someone needs help I am going to help. Along the road of helping you face a lot of difficulties. You think, I'm okay with that. I am willing to take the risk. When you do that, bodhicitta's activity is not comfortable. It's a rocky journey. If you are willing to take that risk, then I think the first seed of bodhicitta is growing in your mind.
>
> I thought this time in Bodhgaya I would like to take the bodhisattva vow again. One evening I went to the Stupa around 5:00 PM, the best time for me. I circumambulated around the Stupa one time, two times, and the third time under the Bodhi Tree, at the exact spot where Buddha became enlightened, when I was there taking the Bodhisattva vow one Bodhi leaf fell from the tree, touched my head and went

down. On both sides of the path people were sitting, chanting, meditating. I thought they were practicing but in fact they were waiting for a bodhi leaf to fall. When the leaf touched the ground from both sides about ten hands reached out and came together. But the leaf was in front of me and my hand went down automatically. My hand was faster than theirs so I touched the leaf and their hands landed on top of mine. I got the leaf.

I felt very good, WOW. The moment I took the vow the leaf touched my head and now I have the leaf. So, feeling very good, I walked a little bit. After one or two seconds I felt very bad. Three seconds ago, I wanted to take a vow for all sentient beings. I wanted to give my life for all sentient beings, but right now I cannot give one leaf to them. So I took the leaf and thought I am a terrible person. There was a very strong contradiction in my mind. I almost smashed the Bodhi leaf. Then a second voice came and said, no, no, maybe this could serve as a good reminder for bodhicitta practice. So, I took the leaf, enclosed it in paper. Now it hangs in my bedroom behind my bed.

The real authentic feeling of bodhicitta is not easy to achieve, but once you have that then you can really do something. I am still working on that. It is very hard. We are always selfish. I want to feel good, I want to chant mantras for my sake, I want to sit down, peace, peace for me. I want to do some tonglen. I want to feel good. Last night I didn't sleep so well. Now I sit down, I give my Dharma, my virtue to all those suffering. After 25 minutes, WOW I feel great. So all Dharma is all about me. I want to feel great, including bodhicitta and taking refuge to the Dharma, Buddha, Sangha. Please protect me. There's always a me behind everything. If we cannot transform that me, Dharma is not going to work at all. Sometimes I go to the Stupa and sometimes I feel sad because all those hundreds of thousands of

> people going around the stupa are carrying their own "me." Me doing prostrations, me chanting, Dharma helping me, me, me. I see very few with no me. Let go of me. Hah. Let go of Dharma. Behind there is a doer, experiencer, practitioner. If that "er" doesn't transform, Dharma is not going to take root in the human mind. It's all about me. Until you let go of that, real bodhicitta will not happen.[9]

Before leaving Bodhgaya, I told Rinpoche I would like to spend more time with two of my other teachers, Jigme Khyentse Rinpoche and Dzongsar Khyentse Rinpoche. He said the Khyentses are both great teachers, but really you should know what you are doing by now. You just need to take refuge, raise bodhicitta, then do some guru yoga. If you can, try to stay in rigpa during your sadhana practice. If not, after the dissolution of the deity, rest in rigpa. Then dedicate the merit. Tsoknyi Rinpoche's approach to Dharma is always very simple and straightforward—recognize rigpa and rest there. That was the heart of all practice. It seemed he never worried much about all the elaborations of sadhana practice.

There is a particular teaching Tsoknyi Rinpoche has given on a number of occasions that I would like to share. I have found this practice especially helpful during difficult times. I have received these teachings both privately and in public. In a Renunciation Retreat given in Crestone, Colorado, Rinpoche described some of the signs that indicate when your lung (prana or wind) is out of balance and the moving upward prana is giving us trouble. A general sign is a busy feeling in the body, a feeling that we want to move, feeling restless and agitated. Underlying that feeling is a sense of fear, but you don't know why. You might be afraid of light or have difficulty being fully present. Rinpoche condensed in a few words the sense of a healthy and balanced prana as feeling clean, open, and having guts and an unbalanced state as cloudy, tight and fearful. Other signs of imbalance might include a dry tongue and lips, pain in different parts of the body, an inability to express yourself well and

---

9   Filmed interview from *Never Give Up: The Heart of Compassion*. James Gritz and Maria Fernanda Rivero, India, 2011.

not being able to just sit down and relax. In general, you might be feeling depressed and lacking in energy or inspiration.

Rinpoche says:

> The first thing we need to do is locate lung's buzz with our conceptual mind. Make this connection in a relaxed manner through the practice of long, slow breathing. Keep mindfulness on the movement of the breath as it locates lung and makes a connection with it. Then, in an equally relaxed manner, begin a mental scan of how lung feels. When you have a clear picture of this, begin to gently bring lung down with the help of the breath, slowly breathing in and out. This soft breathing practice is called "jam lung" and is a traditional practice for working with the subtle body. It acts like a French press coffee maker, using the movement of breath to gently bring the energy of lung down through the body to below the navel.
>
> Jam lung is very simple to do. Relax and take long in-breaths, encouraging the body to rest loosely. Then the conceptual mind can examine the body to see where lung's speediness is active. We find the points where there is tension and tightness, indicating the presence of speediness. As we breathe in the press goes down, connecting with lung wherever we find it. The moment the mind locates the speedy buzz it's already making a relationship with it. When we're ready for the next breath we exhale and begin again. Eventually, we're able to bring lung smoothly down below the navel. Upward-moving lung cannot find its own way home if mind doesn't escort it down. By doing jam lung correctly over and over, restless lung can become normal as it enters the central channel and returns to its home below the navel.
>
> It's very important to establish this collaboration between conceptual mind and the speedy energy of lung; otherwise we might do jam lung practice with our speedy minds and remain out of touch with lung. It may take a while to get it all together, so have

patience and persistence, giving plenty of time to jam lung during practice. If we do jam lung slowly and mindfully as part of our daily practice, lung will definitely learn to stay down. If we train like this for one, two or more months, we'll naturally know when lung is down or not and when it starts to move up. When we feel lung is down, all the big muscles in the body loosen up and we feel quite light. With lung staying in its home, even when we're doing a lot, we won't suffer from buzzy, speedy lung. In post meditation, during which we maintain the mood of meditation, it's good to keep about 10% of the energy below the navel with slight muscle pressure above and below lung's home. This helps gently keep the energy down and enables us to function well in the world. With 10% of the energy held below the navel we can breathe normally, our minds can function normally, and we can get on with whatever we're doing.[10]

This practice of bringing the lung down and holding the breath below the navel is not much different from vase breathing. Even though it is a simple practice it has profound effects. I believe it is a good precursor for the more complex practice of *tummo*.[11] In my own experience, I find that after bringing the lung down and holding the breath below the navel for twenty to fifty times I feel more grounded and spacious. It is much easier to rest in rigpa or at least formless meditation after performing this practice.

---

10 Personal notes from Tsoknyi Rinpoche teachings at a Renunciation Retreat given in Crestone, Colorado, Rinpoche circa 2003. Here is a link to another talk by Tsoknyi Rinpoche on the Jam Lung practice: https://www.meditatorswindimbalance.org/advice-page/advice-on-the-path-tsoknyi-rinpoche/

11 Tummo is the practice of inner heat from the Six Yogas of Naropa. To begin to study this practice you first practice holding the breath below the navel.

Dzogchen Ponlop Rinpoche

Dzogchen Ponlop Rinpoche, circa 2002.

Dzogchen Ponlop Rinpoche is also the teacher of my oldest son, Rishone. It was through my son's prompting that I attended my first teaching with Ponlop Rinpoche at the Boulder Shambhala Center. He was teaching on Garab Dorje's *Three Words that Strike the Vital Point* along with Patrul Rinpoche's famous commentary. Ponlop Rinpoche is another contemporary teacher with a great command of the English language and good grasp of the western mind. Along with his intense education as a tulku in the Kagyu and Nyingma lineages, he also studied at Columbia University.

Ponlop Rinpoche grew up at Rumtek monastery in Sikkim. Rumtek is the seat of the Gyalwang Karmapa. Ponlop Rinpoche's father, Dhamchö Yongdu, was the general secretary of the 16th Karmapa. Ponlop Rinpoche is one of the heart sons of the 16th Karmapa. His root teacher is Khenpo Tsultrim Gyamtso Rinpoche, though he has studied with Dilgo Khyentse Rinpoche, Tulku Urgyen, Nyoshul Khen Rinpoche, Alak Zenkar Rinpoche, and others.

Rinpoche's teachings on Garab Dorje's famous work were clear and inspiring. The Three Words that Strike the Vital Point are pith instructions of Dzogchen view, meditation, and action. The first vital point is the direct introduction to the nature of your mind. You let go and relax in a natural, uncontrived way. As Ponlop Rinpoche explains in his book *Mind Beyond Death* (2008),

> The first word is to *decide directly on one thing*. What are we deciding on? We are deciding that this very moment of consciousness is self-liberated; these very experiences of emotions—of suffering and happiness that are arising—are the expression of rigpa, our naked awareness. We have to ascertain this. We are at least affirming our intention to understand the nature of mind and work toward genuine realization. This decision is the first word that strikes the vital point. The busy mind needs to rest and settle in its true nature. Whatever forms we see with our eyes we let go and relax without naming or conceptualizing what we see. Buddha even taught this in the sutras. When you see, just see it, when you hear, just hear it, and so on.
>
> The second vital point is *recognizing one's true nature*. This is the meditation or sustaining the view. We become directly introduced to rigpa, the essential nature of our mind. We recognize that, apart from this very experience of nowness, this very mind, there is nothing to be pointed out. We recognize that this is it. No matter who appears in front of you—all the buddhas of the ten directions and the

three times, or an ocean of bodhisattvas, dakas and dakinis—there is nothing more to point out. Coming to that kind of recognition is the second word that strikes the vital point.

The third word is to *gain confidence in liberation*. This refers to confidence in self-liberation. We gain confidence that this very mind that we are experiencing now, in this present moment, is self-liberated. When we look directly at that mind, we spontaneously know it as unborn, and we can taste the experience of realization. Developing confidence in that is known as the third word that strikes the vital point.[1]

At the end of his talk there was a period of questions and answers. I asked Ponlop Rinpoche why he didn't give us the pointing out instructions then and there by shouting "Phet". He said, "Why don't you do it." It was an embarrassing moment, but that was the beginning of our connection as teacher and student.

That week I had an interview with Ponlop Rinpoche and I recognized that unique combination of awareness and compassion that I have seen in genuine teachers. I felt during that interview that I was having the nature of mind pointed out without Rinpoche making any big deal about it. His relaxed, clear, and confident presence was enough. I slowly became involved with Ponlop Rinpoche and the Boulder Nalandabodhi sangha. I later discovered that my interview was not the first time I had met Ponlop Rinpoche.

One day when looking through a box of old photographs. I came across a picture I had taken during the first or second visit of His Holiness the 16th Karmapa to Boulder. He was an avid fan of miniature horses. On one occasion we went to a farm with Karmapa to visit their miniature horses, and Ponlop Rinpoche was in his retinue. I believe Ponlop Rinpoche was 16 years old at the time of this photograph. I have a feeling this might have established the karmic link that led to Ponlop Rinpoche becoming one of my close teachers in the future.

---

[1] You can find thorough teachings on "Three Words that Strike the Vital Point" in Dilgo Khyentse's book, *Primordial Purity: Oral Instructions on the Three Words That Strike the Vital Point*. Boulder, CO: Shambhala Publications, 2016.

Pith Instructions from my Teachers

Dzogchen Ponlop Rinpoche and
His Holiness the 16th Karmapa, Boulder, CO, circa 1990.

In 2002, I was with a group of students going on pilgrimage to India with Ponlop Rinpoche. The itinerary was to visit the sacred sites from the life of the Buddha along with stops to visit the 17th Karmapa and Tai Situ Rinpoche. An optional extension on the third week to visit the caves of Ellora and Ajanta in southern India was offered.

We arrived in New Delhi and stayed at the five-star Intercontinental Hotel. I had already been to India a number of times traveling the Buddhist circuit, including Bodhgaya, Vaishali, and

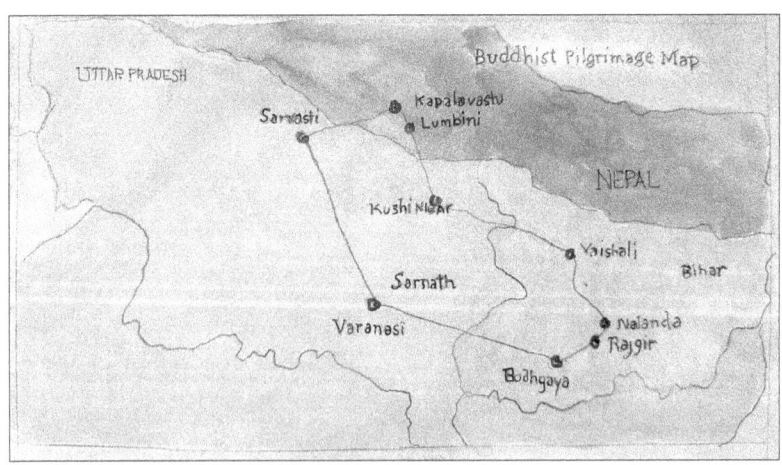

Our pilgrimage route.

Rajgir and Nalanda in Bihar, Sarnath in Varanasi, Shravasti and Kushinagar in Uttar Pradesh, Kapilavastu and Lumbini in Nepal. Except for the ruins of Nalanda University, all the other sites are from the historic life of the Buddha. Usually, I stayed in smaller guest houses or less expensive hotels. The Intercontinental was a luxurious way to start off on what was bound to be a rigorous journey. India is a beautiful and magical land and a feast for a photographer, but between the poverty, dirt, noise, and chaos it can wear you down.

The next day we loaded onto two buses and traveled 10 hours north to Palpung Sherab Ling, in the state of Himachal Pradesh. Sherab Ling is the monastery of Tai Situ Rinpoche. Tai Situ is second in importance in the Karma Kagyu school. I had met Tai Situ Rinpoche many years before when he taught in Boulder Colorado. In 1992, Tai Situpa discovered a "prediction letter" in an amulet the 16th Karmapa had given him. The letter described where to locate the young 17th Karmapa, Orgyen Trinley Dorje. Karmapa has said that studying with Tai Situ Rinpoche was one reason that motivated him to escape from China. The Situpa incarnations (one of the oldest lineages of tulkus) have always been in close relationship to the Karmapas. There is a prophecy portrayed in a painting by Chogkyur Lingpa depicting the 17th Karmapa and Situ Rinpoche sitting in a garden together.

Shortly after arriving at Sherab Ling we had a group audience with Tai Situ Rinpoche. He gave a red hat empowerment and then a teaching. In this teaching, Situ Rinpoche said:

> Whatever you are doing for your practice it should be for the nature of mind. When something dramatic happens, something that doesn't happen every day, it could be some good thing or even some terrible thing, if we are able to apply our meditation when that thing happens then there is a good chance to recognize the nature of mind. For example, you are in a train and somebody takes your wallet which has all your ID's, all your checks, everything. That is very serious, no? Especially if you are in someone else's country. So, that would be a very big shock. When that happens you look at your mind. It's not the

day-to-day mind. It is noticeably different. So you are able to keep your cool and maintain awareness. Look at that mind. I think you will see something.

Of course, please don't try that intentionally. But if something like that happens and these days anything can happen, the shock—the positive shock, the negative shock—instead of getting overwhelmed you keep your cool and watch your state of mind at that stage. You will see something, but I am sure you will be the same person. You will not become Buddha, but you will recognize something. Recognizing the nature of mind and Buddhahood are different, but you will be convinced that you are Buddha. You have no limitation in your essence. Your nature is perfect, your essence is perfect. It's a good thing. When you have a taste of it, it makes a whole lot of difference.

When you learn about it, when you hear about it, it sounds good. But when you really have a taste of it, then it stays with you, and that can only progress. That memory will never fade because it is the beginning of realization. That is why we try so hard to recognize the nature of mind.[2]

Regarding the nature of mind Ponlop Rinpoche said this: "No matter what we experience, one should look at the nature of our minds." For this reason it is said in Vajrayana that an instant makes the difference. Buddhahood is achieved in an instant. The instant we recognize the nature of our mind we are a Buddha.

It has been said that if we recognize that nature of mind we are a Buddha; not recognizing the nature of mind we are an ordinary samsaric being. Through being enslaved to the habitual patterns of our mind we will continue to cycle through the six realms. Once we recognize the nature of mind we are truly on the Vajrayana path.

From Sherab Ling we traveled to Tso Pema (Lotus Lake) in Rewalsar. When we arrived and got off the buses, Ponlop

---

2   Personal notes from teaching by Tai Situ Rinpoche, Sherabling Monastery, India, 2002.

View of Tso Pema (Lotus Lake) in Rewalsar, India, circa 2002.

Rinpoche told us the story of Padmashambhava and the princess Mandarava. According to the story, Guru Rinpoche was teaching Mandarava tantra in the secret Maratika cave when she became his consort. When Mandarava's father, the king of Zahor, found out, he was furious. Padmasambhava and Mandarava were arrested. Mandarava was put in a cell. The king ordered his servants to burn Guru Rinpoche alive. They set him on fire on a funeral pyre in the valley. The fire blazed for a full week and covered the sky with black smoke. When seeing that the black smoke never cleared, they returned to see what had happened. They found Padmasambhava sitting on a giant lotus in the middle of a lake.

One of the blessings of being on pilgrimage with your teacher is to hear the Buddhist stories of the past and to practice and make offerings at the holy sites. When I traveled the Buddhist circuit without the teacher in the past, I often felt a bit lost. Now that I am at this sacred site what do I do besides take pictures? The teacher is always the director in this magical play.

We took the path up to Maratika cave. Here, we practiced a Guru Rinpoche sadhana, Kunchok Chido, and had a small Tsok (feast offering). Ponlop Rinpoche then gave a brief talk. He said we make our aspirations here so we can practice the same way Guru Rinpoche and Madarava did and realize the same nature of mind which is bliss and emptiness. We could realize Mahasuka, or great bliss through the path of Vajrayana—through the path of Dzogchen and Mahamudra. We sat in silence and made our aspirations.

Sarnath, India, 2002.

From Tso Pema, we went to Dharamsala to visit the 17th Karmapa. At Gyuto Monastery the Karmapa gave a long-life empowerment and a guru yoga practice of the 16th Karmapa. Thanks to Ponlop Rinpoche we then had a private audience in the Karmapa's quarters. I will speak more about this later in the section on the Karmapas.

During this 2002 trip I spent a couple of days at the Intercontinental Hotel in New Delhi, which left me euphoric. In fact, the hotel not long ago changed its name to the Eros Hotel. The bed in my opulent room was large enough to sleep four people and had huge fluffy pillows. The hotel had four or five restaurants offering a variety of cuisines, a welcome change from the road food of India. It was a great place to recover from days of long bus rides and taxi trips. After two days luxuriating in this oasis, we flew to Varanasi, the city of lights. We stayed the night in Varanasi and then went to Sarnath, the site where the Buddha turned the first wheel of Dharma.

We wandered the ruins and then settled in front of the Dhamek Stupa where we recited praises to the Buddha. Sarnath, also known as deer park, is the place where the Buddha gave his first teachings on the "Four Noble Truths" after his enlightenment. There is actually a fenced area with Indian deer. As legend has it, in a previous incarnation the Buddha was a deer and offered

Street at night, Varanasi, 2002.

his life to a king who was planning to kill a doe. The king was so touched by the future Buddha's generosity he created the park as a refuge for deer.

I stayed after Rinpoche and the group returned to Varanasi to photograph Sarnath at sunset. When I left the gates of Sarnath all the taxis were gone. I ended up taking a moto-rickshaw. It was a bizarre hour's ride back through the dust and headlights of trucks and cars frantically heading to Varanasi. Coming from the peaceful and sacred side where the Buddha first taught, returning to Varanasi was a powerful entrance into samsara.

We spent another day in Varanasi and then headed to Bodhgaya in the Indian State of Bihar. Bodhgaya is the place where the Buddha attained enlightenment—the heart of Buddhist faith and pilgrimage. It was here on the night of the full moon, under the Bodhi tree more than 2500 years ago that Siddhartha reached the goal of complete enlightenment. Freed from attachment to the habitual patterns and the conditioning of deluded beings he became a Buddha, an awakened one. He abandoned the belief in a truly existent self and accomplished the true state of non-duality. It is said that this is the place where all Buddhas attain enlightenment. Little wonder that Bodhgaya has become the center of Buddhist pilgrimage for devoted pilgrims from all over the world.

Once you enter the inner surroundings of the Mahabodhi temple you enter a magical atmosphere of faith and devotion. Set among the beautiful gardens and sculptures of bodhisattvas and

Mahabodhi Stupa, Bodh Gaya, India, 2002.

realized beings rises the incredible Mahabodhi Temple. Fifty-two meters high, made of sandstone, it points to the sky. In the main shrine temple, it houses the golden statue of the Buddha, considered to be the closest representation of the actual Buddha. Inside this chamber and all around the grounds you will find people practicing meditation, doing prostrations, taking refuge, chanting mantras, and praying with hearts full of devotion. You will find pilgrims and monks from Cambodia, Thailand, Vietnam, China, and Japan. Pilgrims who practice Theravada, Mahayana and Vajrayana Buddhism. If you circumambulate the temple most likely you will pass Tibetan Rinpoches, and teachers and masters from all countries.

Here you will encounter the *vajra asana*, the vajra seat where the Buddha sat under the bodhi tree. For Buddhists the bodhi tree represents the sacred space of enlightenment. It was here where the Buddha sat with unflinching determination to free himself

Inner sanctum of the Stupa at the Mahabodhi Temple, Bodh Gaya, 2002.

from the karma of cyclic existence. Here, in the presence of the bodhi tree and the Mahabodhi temple you can take the ultimate refuge in Buddha, Dharma, and Sangha. You can aspire to achieve the same awakening as the Buddha, who was also a human being like us who went beyond the obscurations of ordinary existence.

Bodhgaya presents a strange juxtaposition between peace and chaos, compassion and suffering, wealth and utter poverty. Walking the half kilometer from the Mahayana guest house, where we stayed, to the Mahabodhi temple grounds you pass feral dogs and cows eating their way through piles of waste on sides of the street. Subaru and Toyota SUVs loaded with lamas jockey for position with bicycle rickshaws on the way to the stupa. Modern buses unload their Chinese, Korean, Indian, and Western tourists to join the continuous flow of pilgrims.

Reaching the promenade leading to the entrance of the Mahabodhi stupa and the sacred bodhi tree you are accosted by child vendors selling incense, candles, and lotus flowers. There is a long row of vendors selling anything from magazines to bodhi leaves. You pass the beggars, cups in hand beckoning for your rupees. On one occasion walking to the Temple, a beggar crawled backward in front of me. He used his hands for feet, his legs gnarled like tree roots from a childhood deformity. One man was leaning against the fence of the temple grounds resting on his armless torso, balancing with the stubs left of his legs. I was told that many families deliberately maim and deform their children as infants so they can be more effective in collecting alms. Here, bordering the sacred site where the Buddha attained transcendent wisdom, you could drown in the ocean of samsara. It is no wonder that after realizing the nature of reality the Buddha taught the truth of suffering.

Entering the gates to the temple grounds you are stuck with the scale and magnificence of the Mahabodhi Stupa. It looks like an ancient spaceship waiting to travel to another realm. It is called the Great Awakening Temple. Next to where the temple now stands is where the Buddha attained enlightenment under the bodhi tree. When the temple was built remains somewhat of a mystery. It is said that the Mahabodhi Temple was built by Emperor Ashoka around 260 BCE but other estimates range from the second to the tenth century CE.

Huge pipal tree facing the Mahabodhi Temple, Bodh Gaya, 2002.

'Self-arising' Tara in small alcove,
Mahabodhi Temple, Bodh Gaya, 2002.

The peace of this revered home of pilgrimage presents such relief and contrast to the desperation outside. I began by circumambulating the stupa on the upper kora path. Under a huge pipal tree facing the temple, monks and lay people are doing prostrations.

Returning to the steps that descend to the temple devotees are offering mandalas and incense. On the left, inside the small alcove pilgrims sit and pray in front of a 'self-arising' Tara.

At the bottom of the stairs, one enters the inner sanctum of the stupa. It houses a colossal statue of the seated Buddha. It is said the statue was made during the time of the historic Buddha and is the closest likeness that exists. It was here with Ponlop Rinpoche the following day that we renewed our refuge and bodhisattva vows. Outside the temple, we sat under the Bodhi tree, a direct descendant of the original tree under which Buddha attained enlightenment. We chanted the king of aspiration prayers.

The bodhi tree is a symbol of Buddha's enlightenment. It was here that the Buddha sat refusing to move until attaining enlightenment. I pray that someday I will have such resolve.

The next day our group crossed the Nairanjana River and stopped at the place where Buddha practiced austerities for six years with his five ascetic followers. It was near here, in the village of Senani that the Buddha was offered rice milk and kusha grass from the Brahmin girl, Sujata.

We climbed the path on the hillside to the Mahakala caves (Dungeshwari cave). There are three caves. It is believed Siddhartha meditated in the central cave. In this cave we offered candles, meditated and made some monetary donations. There is a statue of the emaciated Buddha in meditation posture. Another cave contains a golden Buddha. A statue of Hindu goddess Dungeshwari is also found in the cave temple.

The next day we traveled to Nalanda and Rajgir. Nalanda is the largest excavated ruins of a university in the world, located about two hours from Bodhgaya. It was founded in the fifth century. A great deal of the teaching in Mahayana and Vajrayana came from the scholars of Nalanda, like Shantarakshita, Kamalashila, Chandrakirti, Nagarjuna, and Naropa. Much of the Madhyamika philosophy comes from the teachers of Nalanda. From here we went to Rajagriha. There are two ways to get to Vulture Peak. One is a long uphill hike. The other is to take a cable car to a high up point and walk from there. Most of us chose the long hike. Near the top, there are caves where Ananda and Shariputra lived and practiced the Buddha's teachings. From there it is a short walk to the teaching site at Vulture Peak. There is a rock outcrop that resembles a vulture. From the teaching platform there is a view in all directions of what was once the kingdom of Rajgir.

Ponlop Rinpoche spoke of its significance to Buddhist practitioners. He said:

Vulture Peak, Bihar, India, 2002.

Vulture Peak is the most sacred place for the Mahayana because this is the place where Buddha turned the wheel of the *Prajnaparamita Sutra*. This is the place where he taught not only the Prajnaparamita but also many other mahayana sutras were taught in this region. This is the place where many arhats, bodhisattvas, and mahasiddhas achieved the realization of emptiness (*shunyata*) after Buddha taught the empty nature of reality. Therefore, it is a very profound space. It is important to see after visiting all these sacred places that the great master

Pith Instructions from my Teachers

Shakyamuni Buddha was a human teacher. These are the places where Buddha walked. These are the places where he went for alms, and these are the places where he enlightened many other sentient beings. To have this opportunity to walk in the footsteps of the Buddha is a very profound experience.

It has been an important opportunity for us to see His Holiness Karmapa, the Buddha of our time. The important thing here is to bring all our intellectual studies of the Dharma to the experience which His Holiness taught in Dharamsala. Coming to these places it becomes real.[3]

After our stay in Bodhgaya, we returned to Delhi. From here many of the students returned to their home countries. Others of us stayed to continue with Rinpoche to the caves of Ellora and Ajanta. To get there we flew to Mumbai and then traveled by bus to Aurangabad. In the following days, we visited the magical and majestic cave temples of Ajanta and Ellora.

---

3   Personal notes of talk by Dzogchen Ponlop Rinpoche at Vulture Peak Mountain, Rajgir, India, 2002.

Statues in cave temples of Ajanta, Maharashtra Province, India, 2002.

Painting in cave temples of Ajanta, Maharashtra Province, India, 2002.

Ajanta, one hundred kilometers north from Aurangabad, is one of the artistic wonders of the world. It is a World Heritage site. Ajanta was an active Buddhist center of the seventh century. The paintings of the cave walls illustrate scenes from the Buddha's previous lives as a Bodhisattva. Some of the paintings, especially those of the cave ceilings, depict scenes of everyday life, mixing the magical and mundane.

In various caves one finds the story of the Buddha's birth and life as prince Siddhartha, his temptations by Mara and her voluptuous daughters in Bodhgaya, his enlightenment under the Bodhi tree, and twenty-three huge statues representing the Parinirvana (cave 26). Sravakayanists excavated the first five of the twenty-eight caves. These caves are the most austere, containing columned halls and monk's quarters with rock cut beds. Consistent with Hinayana beliefs there are no stone representations of the Buddha. Hinayana Buddhists abandoned the area around 250 BCE.

More than a century after the great Buddhist King Ashoka, the Vakataka kings of the fourth century, though Hindu, supported Buddhism. They sponsored the creation of some of the more elaborate and intricately carved caves. Around 450 BCE, Mahayana Buddhists resettled the caves and continued the elaborate excavation. Working from the center outwards in both directions in the horseshoe shaped gorge, they completed the remaining twenty-five caves.

It is no wonder that Ajanta is considered one of the crowning achievements of Indian Buddhist sculpture, architecture, and painting. Of the thirty caves, five are Chaitya halls or shrines (9, 10, 19, 26, 29) dedicated to the Buddha, and the rest are viharas, monasteries once used by monks for meditation and study. At one time every inch of the inside of the Mahayana cave walls were painted with murals depicting the lives of the Buddha. Though much of the paint has now peeled off revealing rock face, Ajanta still represents one of the best examples of Indian wall painting.

Today Ajanta is heavily frequented by tourists and is well guarded by the Indian government. Inside the caves the light is dim and it is difficult to see the beauty of what remains of the cave paintings in all their color and detail. Tripods and flash are not allowed so photography is a daunting task. At times a guard will hold up a broken piece of mirror outside the cave reflecting sunlight onto the sculptures of the Buddhas for the benefit of the tourists.

Ellora is located about 30 kilometers northwest of Aurangabad on the ancient trade route connecting the interior of the state of Maharashtra with the western coast of India. In all there are thirty-three caves carved into the hillside of volcanic rock. The first 12 caves were created by Buddhists in Gupta times, 17 caves are Hindu and the remaining four are Jain. The centerpiece is the Kailasa Shiva Temple created around 757-790 CE. It is a copy of the complex Virupaksha temple at Pattadakal and depicts scenes from Shiva and Vishnu Puranas, Ramayana and Mahabharata.

It is believed that the builders of Ajanta moved southwest relocating and creating the caves of Ellora in the early seventh century. The Buddhist caves, all belonging to the Mahayana period, include representations of Sakyamuni Buddha, the five Dhyana Buddhas and various Bodhisattvas and *gandharvas* (celestial beings). The

Cave temple of Ellora, Maharashtra Province, India, 2002.

sculptures and carvings are exquisitely and delicately detailed. The geometric design motifs bordering the doorways and decorating the columns can be found today incorporated in some of the sculptured and painted wood designs in Tibetan monasteries. The Buddhist caves include one Chaitya Hall or temple (cave 10). The other eleven Buddhist caves are viharas with attached monks' quarters. Two of the larger caves are three stories high. The tenth cave, known as the Vishvakarma or carpenters cave houses a large statue of Buddha sitting in front of a thirty foot high stupa. Its large hall is surrounded by two stories of galleries. In the late afternoon around 5:00 PM light shines directly into the cave and moves across the face of the Buddha.

During this pilgrimage, I asked Ponlop Rinpoche if he would give me the *lung* (reading transmission) for the *Lamrim Yeshe Nyingpo* (*Light of Wisdom*). Here, in the tenth cave seated in front of the giant statue of Buddha, Rinpoche gave the *lung* to the group.

As I mentioned earlier the teacher is the magician directing the pilgrimage play. Rinpoche waited until the perfect moment, in the perfect place to give the reading transmission I had requested. The *Lamrim Yeshe Nyingpo* is a terma text revealed by the terton Chokgyur Lingpa. The title is translated as *The Gradual Path of the Wisdom Essence*.' As Erik Pema Kunsang says in his translation,

Giant statue of Buddha in 10th cave of Ellora, Maharashtra Province, India, 2002.

This most precious, concise, profound teaching of Padmasambhava is a condensation of the entire path to enlightenment and, in its full version, it contains the pith instructions of the Three Inner Tantras: Maha, Anu, and Ati yoga.... Praised by Jamyang Khyentse Wangpo as being more valuable than thirty yak loads of scriptures the Lamrim Yeshe Nyingpo, together with the commentary by Jamgon Kongtrul, comprises the important last volume in both the collections of termas and teaching renowned as Ringchen Terdzo and Chokling Tersar.[4]

---

4   Padmasambhava. *The Light of Wisdom*. Translated by Erik Pema Kunsang. Vol. 1. Boudhanath, Hong Kong, and Esby: Rangjung Yeshe Publications, 1999. p. *xxvii*.

Reclining Buddha relief in cave temple of Ellora,
Maharashtra Province, India, 2002.

I feel very fortunate to have received some of these teachings from my teachers and to have the opportunity to continue studying this cycle of teachings.

Ponlop Rinpoche is a very direct and skillfull master. He always seems to have the right answer at the right time and place. I remember a moment in Seattle during the renovation of a Greek Orthodox Church into Nalanda West. I was in the shrine room with Ponlop Rinpoche. I brought up how difficult the path to enlightenment seems. I mentioned the struggles and work Milarepa had endured to attain realization. His last teaching to Gampopa was to pull down his pants and show Gampopa the calluses on his ass from meditation. Rinpoche said, "And what was all that for? To relax."

From an interview for my documentary, *Never Give Up*,
filmed in Bodhgaya, India, circa 2009.

In 2009 in Bodhgaya, while filming our documentary on the Karmapa, Ponlop Rinpoche kindly granted us an interview. For me this interview was a pith instruction on the path.

> The realization of the nature of mind doesn't really depend on any outer forms. Be it a cushion, a certain type of retreat or any kind of ritual. It doesn't depend on that. The realization of the nature or mind, or awakening needs three things. It needs your participation. It needs a good guide, spiritual friend, a teacher, and then the instruction. That's all. And then you have to do it. You can do it anywhere. It doesn't matter. It can be in Gritz studio. Right? Ah, that's Mahamudra.... I think the most important thing is not to look too far away. Yeah, don't look too far. Whatever you are looking for is right there. Close to you. The farther you fly away you have a lesser chance of finding it.[5]

---

5   James Gritz and Maria Fernanda Rivero. *Never Give Up: The Heart of Compassion.* India, 2011.

Dzongsar Khyentse Rinpoche

Dzongsar Khyentse Rinpoche

Dzongsar Khyentse Rinpoche, also known as Khyentse Norbu the filmmaker, is considered a very high incarnation. He was recognized by His Holiness Sakya Trizin as the incarnation of the great Jamyang Khyentse Chökyi Lodrö, and an incarnation of Jamyang Khyentse Wangpo and an emanation of Manjushri. Orgyen Tobgyal Rinpoche said in Deer Park in Bir India, "It follows quite naturally to say that Dzongsar Khyentse Rinpoche is Manjushri for our time; the living, breathing embodiment of the wisdom of all the Buddhas of the ten directions and three times.

Pith Instructions from my Teachers

Dilgo Khyentse Rinpoche, Rocky Mountain Dharma Center, Colorado, 1976.

I first encountered Rinpoche when he came at a young age and gave a talk at Karma Dzong after the death of Trungpa Rinpoche. I believe he was there at the request of Dilgo Khyentse Rinpoche to help calm the conflicted Vajradhatu community. Since then I have attended many of Rinpoche's teachings given in Canada, Australia, Mexico, the U.S. and India.

Dzongsar Khyentse Rinpoche is the most outwardly outrageous of my living teachers from a conventional worldly point of view. He has no qualms about stirring up a public hornet's nest. All you have to do is read some of the posts on his facebook page.¹ In spite of this he is probably the strictest teacher I know when it comes to presenting Vajrayana teachings. I believe that his root teacher Dilgo Khyentse Rinpoche told him not to teach Vajrayana until he was 50. Before then he taught on many subjects like Madhyamika, the bodhisattva path, bardo, the *Uttara Tantra*, Manjushri, Mahayana sutras, Nagarjuna, *Prajnaparamita Sutra*, *Words of My Perfect Teacher*, and so many more.

Dzongsar Khyentse Rinpoche likes to present certain important teachings on all continents. Like his previous incarnation Jamyang Khyentse Wango, he feels it is his duty to preserve and propagate the teachings of the Buddha from all schools of Tibetan Buddhism true to the Rime style.

When it comes to sharing tantra he can be very strict, adhering to the ancient tradition of keeping many Vajrayana teachings secret. He feels that in many cases it is being taught too openly and can be misinterpreted when given too freely in the wrong context. In some teachings and empowerments, he emphasizes not sharing what he is teaching to anyone outside the group that is presently there. He warns frequently about not sharing on social media.

I would say that to a certain extent all my teachers enforce the secrecy of certain tantric teachings. Yet these days almost all the so-called secret teachings are readily available in books, the internet, and freely given at retreats. Some make the argument that in this dark age which seems to be getting darker and darker that is important to share these teachings. Some of my teachers have given the pointing instructions in open retreats to students new to the Dharma while others keep this very private. I think it must be a difficult decision for a teacher to decide what to share and what not to share. Chögyam Trungpa Rinpoche was like this for most of the time I was his student, but near the end of his life he became more open about sharing and publishing his Vajrayana teachings.

For many traditional gurus, teachings like Mahamudra, Maha Ati, and Dzogchen are not offered until the student has completed all the preliminary practices. This is how Trungpa Rinpoche did it. Because the times have become so difficult, with

---

1   Dzongsar Jamyang Khyentse Facebook Page https://www.facebook.com/djkhyentse

the possibility of nuclear wars, and with global warming bringing so many disasters, I think many teachers have reevaluated what they share.

For example, *Three Words that Strike the Vital Point* is a pivotal text in the Dzogchen teachings. There is really nothing more profound than these teachings by Patrul Rinpoche from Garab Dorje, two of the greatest masters of all time. These teachings have been published in the book *Primordial Purity* (2016) by His Holiness Dilgo Khyentse Rinpoche, a root guru of all my teachers.

The Flight of the Garuda by Shabkar Lama also contains deep pith instructions on Dzogchen. It was once a restricted text but there is a translation by Keith Dowman now available from Amazon.[2]

Deciding on a guru is not always a simple matter. Dzongsar Khyentse Rinpoche emphasizes the importance of investigating the teacher before becoming involved, especially with a Vajrayana master. It is important for both the student and the teacher to evaluate the relationship, the bond between teacher and student before jumping in and making the commitment to the tantric path. A sacred bond is made between guru and disciple, the samaya vow. I spoke of this earlier. From what I have been taught, once you have entered the Vajrayana path there is no turning back without grave consequences. It is often said that Hinayana and Mahayana are much safer paths, but it is also said that on those paths it may take eons before attaining enlightenment. It is possible to obtain realization in one lifetime on the path of tantra.

The goal of the guru is to make the student self-reliant. Dzongsar Khyentse Rinpoche has even given a talk on becoming your own master. As it is said so many times you have Buddha nature, there is nothing you need to find outside yourself. This is your inner guru, and this is what the outer guru works so hard to have you realize. He said, "Then if you ask me, then why do we need the guru? Because you want the enlightenment fast, that's why. It's as easy as that."

I think being a genuine guru is the hardest and most demanding job in the world. For this alone I bow down at the feet of all my teachers. The training of Rinpoches is extensive beginning at an

---

2   Keith Dowman, trans. *The Flight of the Garuda: The Dzogchen Tradition of Tibetan Buddhism*. 2nd ed. Somerville, MA: Wisdom Publications, 1994.

early age. Usually, they are raised by an attendant and educated by a Khenpo (a teacher with degree for higher Buddhist studies. The Tibetan version of a PhD). Once they become teachers they travel the world giving seminars and retreats. Even during the breaks at a retreat they are usually giving private or group interviews. Once a Tantric teacher takes on a student he makes the vast commitment of guiding the student to enlightenment for as many lifetimes as it takes.

The sheer arduousness of the Vajrayana training to get to the level of Rinpoche is hard to fathom. Their doctrinal and practical education is extensive, often spanning decades, sometimes in demanding conditions. And once they are trained, it seems like their role requires infinite patience for their students and gritty stamina to keep up with their teaching and travel schedules.

In 2000, after teachings in Bodhgaya, I was traveling with my son Arthur to the sacred sites from the life of the Buddha. We traveled from Bodhgaya, where the Buddha attained enlightenment, to Kushinagar, the site of the Buddha's death, Parinirvana and cremation. When we arrived in Kushinagar, Arthur and I walked into a hotel restaurant to have lunch. There, sitting at a large table with a few western students and a small entourage of monks was Dzongsar Khyentse Rinpoche. He was talking about politics. He invited us to come and sit down. Concerning the importance of Kushinagar, Dzongsar Khyentse Rinpoche says,

> Passing into parinirvana is, of all the Buddha's teachings, the one that makes the most impact on our minds, as it transcends all our concepts about birth, old age, sickness, death, time, increasing, decreasing, samsara and nirvana. Those of us who have not yet woken up to our true nature are still bound by time, space, quantity, and speed, unlike those who have entered parinirvana and cannot be bound by any kind of dualistic phenomena.[3]

---

3   *What To Do at India's Buddhist Holy Sites* by Dzongsar Khyentse is available for download as a PDF at "Rinpoche's New Book Available For Download". Khyentse Foundation. https://khyentsefoundation.org/preview-of-rinpoches-new-book-available-for-download/

After lunch, Rinpoche invited us to come to the Parinirvana Stupa with him to make offerings. We went along with the group. Usually, at a sacred place, a teacher or student will buy some candles and light them along with offering flowers. Rinpoche bought all the candles the young Indian boys had to sell, all they could round up. Hundreds of candles were lit.

The aim of all Buddhist practice is to catch a glimpse of the awakened state. Going on pilgrimage, soaking up the sacred atmosphere of holy places and mingling with other pilgrims are simply different ways of trying to achieve that glimpse. While at Kushinagar you can do all the practices you do at the other holy sites, perhaps the most significant one to do here is to contemplate the Buddha's statement about impermanence, and if you know how, to meditate on extremelessness or emptiness.

Light offerings are also very popular and heavy with spiritual symbolism. The reason we follow the Buddha's teachings is that we long to achieve enlightenment, which will only happen once we've tamed or trained our minds. Just as light illuminates the space around it so that others can see, and also illuminates itself, mind not only knows others, but also knows itself. For this reason, a lamp is the closest simile we have to mind, and therefore anything that has the power to dispel darkness can be used as an offering substance.

> I will offer precious lamps,
> Arranged in rows on lotuses of gold,
> A carpet of sweet flowers scattering
> Upon the level, incense-sprinkled ground.[4]

As Arthur and I were traveling in the opposite direction of Rinpoche. The thought crossed my mind perhaps to change our trip and travel with Rinpoche back to Bodhgaya, but I was set on photographing all the sites from the Buddha's life. I had the idea of publishing a coffee table book, so we continued on to Lumbini in Nepal. Perhaps ego took precedence over the auspicious opportunity that was presented. I regret that I didn't change our plans and travel with Rinpoche. We stayed a while with everyone making

---

4   Ibid.

Dzongsar Khyentse Rinpoche circa 2000.

prayers and aspirations, then said goodbye and took our leave to continue towards Lumbini in Nepal to the sacred site where the Buddha was born.

I saw Dzongsar Khyentse Rinpoche again in August of 2001 during the consecration of The Great Stupa of Dharmakaya that Liberates Upon Seeing at the Rocky Mountain Dharma Center. He was surrounded by a lot of people when I approached him. While I stood on the outskirts of the group he reached through the crowd and took my hand saying I got your email. At this point, I can't remember what the email was about but I do remember my complete surprise at his greeting.

Five years later I was in Bodhgaya attending teachings at Shechen Monastery. One day while wandering the grounds of the Mahabodhi Temple I came across a large group of monks in Tibetan robes sitting behind what appeared to be another monk with his robes drawn over his head, all facing the Stupa. I was certain by their comportment they were sitting with their teacher. Approaching a little closer I recognized the "seeming" monk in front as Dzongsar Khyentse Rinpoche. He got up, walked to the Kora path, and circumnambulated the Stupa. I followed a short distance behind him. At one point he turned back towards me and signaled me to go in front of him. I had too much respect for him to pass and walk in front, so I continued to walk behind him. A few minutes later he turned again and said, "walk in front you're blowing my cover."

During that week I had been attending teachings at Shechen monastery by Jigme Khyentse Rinpoche, Dzigar Kongtrul Rinpoche, and Rabjam Rinpoche. Every morning we would go sit facing the Stupa and do our daily practice. One day Matthieu Ricard told a group of students that instead of leaving their shoes at the gate to the Temple, which was the common practice, it was all right if they carried their shoes with them concealed in a bag when doing Kora on the upper level.

When I exited the Stupa grounds and entered the wide pathway with all the vendors and beggars, I saw Dzongsar Khyentse standing alone about ten meters away. I watched as a group of students recognized him and ran to where he was standing. As soon as they arrived, he began castigating them for carrying their shoes in a bag into the sacred grounds of the Stupa, where Buddha had attained enlightenment. Although I had never seen this wrathful aspect of Rinpoche before, the only thought that entered my mind was that I wished I was one of his students being chastised like that.

It is easy to understand that the teacher's time is very precious and limited. They receive many questions from students providing endless details about what is wrong with their relationship with their partners, whether they should move to Seattle or Australia, can the teacher do a *mo* (a divination) about what they should do next with their life, how should they handle their new boss or wife or lover. They act as if the teacher were a fortune teller, marriage counselor, or a therapist.

I too have been guilty of this. Now from my older perspective, I understand that the teacher's job is to teach Dharma, and not to be my buddy, babysitter, daddy or travel agent. I think asking questions other than those related to the Dharma and your practice is wasting the teacher's time. On the other hand, there is no problem engaging in ordinary conversation with your teacher, but I don't think you need to schedule an interview to do so.

I have attended a number of Rinpoche's teaching at the University of British Columbia (UBC) in Vancouver.

During one of Rinpoche's teachings in Vancouver, I was granted an interview. Once in the interview room, Rinpoche signaled me to sit on the floor close to him. I started to mention my email about Bodhgaya but before a few words escaped my mouth he said, "You mean the one with the shoes?" "Yes, that one." I was amazed that out of the tens of thousands of emails he receives, he would remember my stupid email. I then asked if he would accept me as one of his students. He replied that it was good to have a lot of teachers. I went on to say that was fine but I wanted him to be my teacher. Again, he told me in a nonchalant manner as if I was bothering him, it was good to have many teachers, the more the better. I was looking for him to acknowledge some commitment as a Vajra master. I asked him a third time to be my teacher. This time he shouted, "OK!" At that very moment, sitting so close, it seemed his head exploded, light bursting out like in the movie *Cocoon* (1985) when the aliens revealed themselves to the old people in the swimming pool.

In 2008 I was hired by His Holiness Gyalwang Drugpa, the head of the Drukpa Kagyu school, to photograph the Drukpa monasteries in India, Ladakh, Nepal, and Bhutan.

On my trip through Bhutan, as a student of Trungpa Rinpoche it was unthinkable not to visit Taktsang. Taktsang is located on a cliffside in the upper Paro valley in Bhutan. It is called Tiger's Nest and it was here that Padmasambhava revealed the Mandala of Pelchen Dorje Phurpa, The legend says that Guru Rinpoche was carried from Tibet to Taktsang on the back of a tigress, thus giving it the name "Tiger's Nest."

Taktsang is the place where Padmasambhava meditated and manifested in his wrathful form as Dorje Trolö. It was here that Trungpa Rinpoche received the mind terma of the Sadhana of Mahamudra in 1968.

This practice text joins together the teachings of both the Nyingma and Kagyü lineages, merging crazy wisdom and devotion. Crazy wisdom is considered the key to understanding the awakened state of Guru Rinpoche. Trungpa Rinpoche gave two talks on Crazy Wisdom in 1972. In his book *Crazy Wisdom* he examines the life of Padhmasambha.

After riding part way up on horseback and walking the rest of the way on foot I arrived at the monastery. A photo I took of Taktsang is the cover of this book. There are eight caves at the monastery. Once finding the cave where it is said Guru Rinpoche meditated I sat down in a corner and practiced the Sadhana of Mahamudra.

In October we heard that Dzongsar Khyentse Rinpoche was giving the Dudjom Tersar transmission in Bartsham. Kathy and I hired a driver to take us to Chador Lhakhang in Bartsham where the teachings were being held. When we arrived at the Lhakhang we asked about Dzongsar Khyentse Rinpoche. We were directed to a building up a steep hill. We entered a large room where Rinpoche and others were having lunch. The room was full of light, surrounded by windows with views of the mountains. Rinpoche was wearing a large Obama button and there was a political discussion going on. Rinpoche invited us to have lunch. He asked if we thought Obama would win the election. I think I answered that I did not think a black man could be elected as the president of the United States. This was my view at the time.

I have never been good at political predictions, as evidenced again by the fact that I could never have imagined Donald Trump becoming the president. Rinpoche asked me what we were doing in Bhutan. I told him about the project I was working on for Gwalwang Drugpa Rinpoche. I don't remember what he said but I do remember having the distinct impression that he felt little connection with Gyalwang Drugpa.

Rinpoche then prepared a flatbread for Kathy and me to try. He wrapped it in paan or betel leaf. It tasted somewhat strange. Shortly after eating this appetizer, we began feeling a distinct buzz akin to having taken cocaine. We wondered if it was the leaf or just the contact with Rinpoche. I have since read that betel leaf can have a psychoactive effect. Many Indians combine the leaf with areca nut to make a rather disgusting red paste. They use it like chewing tobacco, always spitting it on the street. It stains the teeth red.

After lunch, we returned to the shrine hall where Rinpoche continued the empowerment and teachings. We sat with a Westerner named Wyatt He sat near a larger group of other Westerners. Wyatt was very kind and helpful in orienting us to what was happening. At one point, I needed a bathroom and he directed me to the one in his room. I did not know this at the time but Wyatt was recognized as a tulku by the late Chagdud Tulku.

During the Dudjom Tersar transmission, Rinpoche conveyed a comprehensive picture of the Vajrayana path. Even though Guru Yoga is the last part of the ngöndro, Rinpoche said, since everyone had been reciting the seven-line prayer he would begin his teachings there. He began with the three forms of the guru. The outer guru is the physical guru. He is a human being, not a celestial being or Yidam. He is here walking on the earth; he is touchable and we can easily relate to him. The inner guru is the clarity aspect of mind and the secret guru is the emptiness aspect. Both the outer and secret guru are Buddha nature or the nature of mind. For the Vajrayana practitioner, the guru is the yidam deity, Guru Rinpoche, Vajrasattva, Samantabhadra, or whichever teacher relates to the deity yoga you are practicing.

Referring to the seven-line supplication to Guru Rinpoche, Dzongsar Khyentse Rinpoche explained during his teachings at Bartsham:

> When you practice the Seven Line Prayer, at times you should dissolve the guru into you and remain in that state for a while and look at that state. When we say look, some people expect to see miracles and light. Other people say they see clarity, but this isn't from experience—they're just reciting what they read in a book. This is of no value. Gomchen means great meditator—you have to meditate. There is no need to speak elegantly of your experience. For example, one of HH Dilgo Khyentse Rinpoche's students, a gomchen, was asked to visualize Guru Rinpoche on a lotus. But he had never seen a lotus, and there were small yellow flowers outside the cave where he was meditating, so he visualized that. But Guru Rinpoche's weight was too great, so he fell backward and exposed his private parts. When he told HH Dilgo Khyentse Rinpoche about his experience, he was very happy, as this was a real experience, not something memorized from a book.[5]

I have wondered why the guru yoga practice we are given by the teacher is usually Guru Rinpoche and not the Buddha. Rinpoche explained this in his teaching.

---

5   Personal notes from teachings at Bartsham Dzongsar Khyentse Rinpoche during the Dudjom Tersar empowerments, 2008.

> Why do we visualize Guru Rinpoche and not the Buddha? One of the most important aspects of the view is interdependence, and because of this we have the notion of a "karmic link". Guru Rinpoche is linked to Bhutan and Tibet, the main domains of his activity. Shakyamuni didn't visit Bhutan, but Guru Rinpoche did. And one of Guru Rinpoche's five main consorts was from Bumthang, so even on an outer level there's a link. Guru Rinpoche acts as a mirror for us to look into the nature of our minds.[6]

I hope at the time of death I can remember this teaching he gave while talking about Guru Yoga. The point here is that when you die and are entering the bardo of dying you may not recognize mind's nature and awaken on the spot. Most people pass out before the child luminosity meets the mother luminosity when the white and red tigles (drops of the mother and father principles) join at the heart center. When you wake up you will find yourself tossed around in the bardo like a leaf in the wind. You may not recognize the yidam of your sadhana practice who stands in front of you. You may become terrified of the wrathful deities that appear before you and run right into the god realm or hungry ghost or hell realm. You might see your future parents copulating and seek the comfort of rebirth in the human realm. But many great teachers have said it is less difficult to remember your guru and this in itself will lead to awakening.

In a talk about Guru Yoga during teachings at Bartsham during the Dudjom Tersar empowerments, Dzongsar Khyentse Rinpoche said:

> Why is Guru Yoga the most important practice? When you die, you can only take three things: guru, view, and yidam. What does it mean to bring the view? At the end of the dissolution of the elements, you reach the Chönyi bardo (the bardo of dharmata), and if you have practiced (the view), you'll recognize Dharmakaya and become liberated. But this is very

---

6   Ibid.

Dzongsar Khyentse Rinpoche, Mexico, 2017.

hard, as we're confused and frightened then. It's easier to remember and visualize the yidam if you have practiced, but this is still hard. The easiest of all is to remember the guru, as you have been with your teacher a lot and you have got used to him. If someone recites the guru's name into your ear as you die, you'll easily remember him.[7]

To study this wealth of tantric teachings thoroughly I suggest you do an online search using the prompt: "DJKR teaching during Dudjom Tersar" to find the transcription of the teachings by Lama Sonam Phuntsok.[8] It comprises 51 pages of Rinpoche's Vajrayana

---

7   Ibid.

8   You will find these teachings here: https://www.scribd.com/document/497289507/pdfslide-us-djkr-teachings

teaching from the preliminary practices through the creation and completion stages of Deity yoga. Such comprehensive and pithy teaching is difficult to encounter.

After going through some bouts of depression in 2013 I decided I needed a change to break the cycle and I moved to Mexico. In October of 2017 Dzongsar Khyentse gave a series of public talks in Mexico City which I attended. They were titled *Peyote vs Shamatha vs Vipassana vs Habanero vs Mariachi vs Mojito*.

The talks had little to do with peyote or mojito. The teachings mostly revolved around samatha and vipassana. There was one point where Mariachi's did appear and performed to Rinpoche. During these teachings, Rinpoche gave many guided meditations, mostly for short periods. These teachings revolved around learning to watch the mind and not feed thoughts and emotions, or even itches we might be feeling. The point was to keep our awareness.

Distraction is the fundamental problem. The short sessions were to train us, or at least give us a taste of non-distraction. There were guided meditations on feeling and smell and even chewing and tasting a little food. Rinpoche said,

> When we look at things, we always look at things through the filter, through the veil. Veil of all kinds which we have collected from education, upbringing, culture, habitual—just so many.... Now, to be free from this entanglement is what we call the Buddhist path.
>
> Basically, a very important connotation of *dhyana* is the non-distracted mind. Distraction is the mother of all the emotions. And when I'm talking about distractions, I'm not talking about gross distractions such as browsing the web. Like when you are thinking about something, you don't even know you are thinking that thing.
>
> So, sit straight. And all you have to do is to be aware of what is happening in your mind. Whatever is not in your mind is not a phenomenon. What is happening in your mind is the only phenomenon that you have. So all you have to do is to be aware of

that. And we are not talking about the phenomena of the past. We are not talking about the phenomena of the future. But this moment. And it doesn't have to be special. It doesn't have to be wholesome, spiritual. It can be absolutely mundane and ordinary. So please do that for a few moments.[9]

Rinpoche went on to say that

> ... it is possible to remain non-distracted while drinking tequila on the beach. But for beginners, the chances of becoming distracted are more probable than sitting straight. This mind is longing for distractions. It's craving. It wants to read a story, it wants to go. You understand? It wants to sort of move. When doing a longer practice the mind will long for distractions.[10]

One day my friend Fernanda asked me to photograph the teachings. I had done this in the past at other events. She had not asked me to cover this event but on this day the photographer didn't show up. She had only a rather wide-angle lens on her camera. I told her this would never work at the distance where she had me sitting. She cleared a space for me to sit directly in front of Rinpoche. I was snapping away when I thought maybe I was bothering Rinpoche when he was talking. During a break I asked Rinpoche if I was bothering him. He answered nothing you do bothers me. I don't care if you run around the hall naked.

The next day Rinpoche went on to introduce longer practice times encouraging us to sit straight without scratching, or coughing and also not engaging in whatever thoughts arise. Just watching. With practice we learn to stop feeding our thoughts and the organization of thoughts, the habitual patterns become less. Things that previously excited you calm down. Things that make you angry or agitated are not as strong as they were. "Then, totally,

---

9   Personal notes from Dzongsar Khyentse Rinpoche teachings "Peyote vs Shamatha vs Vipassana vs Habanero vs Mariachi vs Mojito," Mexico City, Mexico, 2017.
10 Ibid.

all the time in the state of peyote." He went on to say, "Most of the people don't even have a shrine or things like that. Like a zafu, a meditation cushion, they are a help for meditation, but they are also a hindrance. You should be able to meditate anywhere, that is the point. Because basically, all you need is mind. You're not visualizing, you're not chanting mantra, no seed syllables, nothing, none of this stuff. Just sit."[11]

Dzongsar Khyentse Rinpoche spoke about the importance of short moments many times, saying,

> This is advice from the Buddha himself and also subsequently many of his lineage holders. Longchenpa of the Nyingma tradition related: like a dripping of water, you should do very short ones but many, many times. Then the bucket will be filled before you even are aware of it. You know it's already filled. It's very good advice, pith instructions.[12]

In January 2019 at the end of a teaching given in Argentina, Dzongsar Khyentse Rinpoche was asked, "How can you recognize your mind as the Buddha, as the Guru?" He answered:

> There are volumes and volumes of answers in the Mahamudra, the Madhyamika, and the Mahasandhi. This is a very big question. But for now, just to answer your question, it's a very big question. This is not even a myth. It's not a philosophy. It's hands on, it's raw. Mind, by function, keeps on knowing. You see, you keep on knowing something. You keep on noticing something. You keep on being aware of something. You always keep on being conscious because of this mind. Yes, sometimes it is so painful that we have a mind. I'm sure sometimes we wish that we were this table—no hope, no fear, comfortably sitting here. No need to make schedules. This table is not thinking, oh does she like me, does he like me.

---

11 Ibid.
12 Ibid.

It doesn't think, oh this hot thing was placed on my head, now this cold thing is placed on my head. But, it's too late, you already have mind.

From one side this is so painful to have mind but if you look at it from the other side it's such a blessing. You have this cognizance. It's incredible. Wow. You have this cognizance. See, just experience it. It's incredible, because of this mind something like this got designed. (pulls on his t-shirt). And shoes, just amazing (picks up his multi-colored shoe and looks at it)—mind made this. Something like this happened. Of course, the Gucci shoes. This is what. (shakes the shoe). What is it called? (translator) Alpargata? Stylish right? See mind thinks like this. If this is not a Buddha what is? But if you don't use it as a Buddha it won't function as a Buddha. It's like, I give you a piece of gold ore, and you don't know anything about gold. And I give you a bag full of ore. You look at it and you think it is garbage and you throw it away. If you don't know how to use it then it will end up producing things like shoes. This mind is so interesting. Like dead leaves, hot water—tea. Beans roasted, crushed, who thought about these things, and put hot water—coffee. Why do people like to eat things that are string-like? Like spaghetti, noodles. We like tasting things that have layers, like one bread, onion, ham cheese, lettuce, so that when we eat, close your mouth and you go through the layers—sandwich. Then, of course, Democracy, Communism—stuff like this. Saraha said, he prostrated to the mind (Rinpoche says in Tibetan). "To the mind that is like a wish-fulfilling jewel, I prostrate to this mind." OK, I think we will end today.[13]

I attended the teachings of Rinpoche in Australia in 2017. On August 4, Rinpoche first gave teachings in Sydney. Before leaving Sydney I was able to go to a screening of Rinpoche's (Khyentse

---

13　Ibid.

Dzongsar Khyentse Rinpoche circa 2017.

Norbu's) new film *Looking for a Lady with Fangs and a Mustache* (2017). There was a social gathering after the film. Rinpoche meandered through the room socializing with fans and students. When he came by, I greeted him. He said hello and then turned his head and in a loud voice called out "Emily, he's here." I have no clue what this meant. When I left before returning to my hotel I wandered around the Sydney harbor somewhat dazed and confused not sure why I was feeling unsettled.

After this, further south at Aloka Meditation center between Sydney and New Castle, a drupchen and empowerments (Chime Phagme Nyingthik, Vima Ladrup and Korwa Dongdruk) were to

Dzongsar Khyentse Institute, Gadiara, Himachal Pradesh, India, 2022.

take place. Because of his schedule Dzongsar Khyentse arrived late to the drupchen and it was led by Jigme Khyentse until he arrived. Orgyen Tobgyal Rinpoche was also present.

Dzongsar Khyentse Rinpoche said:

> A drubpa chenpo, a drupchen, requires all kinds of details. For example, you have to do six sessions, you must have a certain number of yogis and yoginis and the sound of the mantra must never be interrupted. If there's any drupchen happening, one must try to participate. Just as we should participate in tsok offerings again and again, it is really good to participate in a drupchen as a Vajrayana practitioner again and again. It is believed that just going to one drupchen will take care of all samaya breakages instantly. Where there is no drupchen, one should try to organize one.[14]

I always found it remarkable how the various teachers could fill in for each other whenever things did not go as planned, which was often.

---

14 Personal notes from Dzongsar Khyentse Rinpoche teachings, Chime Phagme Nyingthik empowerment, Australia, 2017.

Pith Instructions from my Teachers

Rinpoche teaching at Dzongsar Khyentse Institute, Gadiara, Himachal Pradesh, India, 2022.

In 2022 I attended a Drubthab Kuntu cycle of teachings and initiations in northern India near Bir at the Dzongsar Institute. Before the teachings Rinpoche published a letter of warning about coming to these teachings and wrote:

> But if you still insist on receiving these teachings, then, as someone who worries about the decline of the Buddhadharma in general and especially the Vajrayana, I will try my best to have the participants in my heart. That's because a tantric master must look at each student as their only child, which doesn't mean I will know your first name or keep in regular touch with you. For those of you who still de-

cide to receive these initiations from me after reading this far, I need to tell you that our relationship will change completely. There will be no negotiation, no second-guessing, no give and take, and no sitting on the fence. In this case, the customer is not always right and doesn't get to call the shots. If you want to play football, you may get scratches and bruises. If you want to play the game with a helmet and padding, then it's no longer soccer.

For those in limbo, wondering whether or not they should do this, I suggest following the tantric prescription to do a thorough background check on me. There are plenty of websites you can consult, and you might particularly want to read posts by Tahlia Newland, Matthew Remski, Joanne Clark and others.[15]

The teachings and hundreds of empowerments took place over two months, every day without a break. Over 3,000 people attended from all over the world. Rinpoche taught every day from 8 AM to around 5 PM with a break for lunch. Watching him work so hard giving one short empowerment after another without distraction increased my devotion. For me the long days were difficult. Sitting in a crowded hall for seven or eight hours a day can be exhausting. At times I strained to pay attention to the empowerments and visualizations. Even though masks were required many people got Covid. One day an old Tibetan woman had a heart attack in the shrine room. My friend Keith, who is an emergency doctor from New York, worked hard to save her but she died right there in the shrine hall. In spite of the many obstacles, it was a powerful and magical time. I feel fortunate to have attended.

The whole purpose of the Dharma is to dismantle the protective system we have created for ourselves that we call ego. The purpose behind each syllable of the Dharma and every one of its methods is to contradict, disrupt, and rip that ego apart until the goal of complete liberation from it has finally been achieved.

---

15   Letter by Dzongsar Khyentse Rinpoche posted on Siddhartha's Intent website before a Drubthab Kuntu cycle of teachings and initiations in northern India near Bir at the Dzongsar Institute, 2022.

The 16th and 17th Karmapas

The 16th Karmapa, Rangjung Rigpe Dorje.

I met the 16th Karmapa when he came to Boulder in 1976. He was hosted by Trungpa Rinpoche and the Vajradhatu sangha. I had heard a great deal about the Karmapa before his visit. As the head of the Karma Kagyu school he was extremely important to Trungpa Rinpoche and his followers.

The Karmapa is considered an emanation of the bodhisattva Avalokiteshvara, and the "knower of the three times." He can see in his dreams and visions where tulkus will reincarnate. Karmapa literally means "He who Performs the Activities of the Buddha" and ideally, a Karmapa is a person of action. And the Karmapa is also a kind of servant because he must work or act to benefit others. My time with the 16th and 17th Karmapas proved this emphasis on action to be true.

I think it was during the second or third visit of the Karmapa to Boulder that I was asked to take a photo of Trungpa Rinpoche with the Karmapa and Jamgong Kongtrul Rinpoche, who had accompanied him. In the confines of a small room in Karma Dzong the Karmapa's confidence and compassionate presence was obvious, but still I did not feel the kind of immediate and intimate connection I had felt when meeting Trungpa Rinpoche. Today, recollecting the visits of the 16th Karmapa, I feel maybe he was too vast and abstract for my young mind to grasp.

Pith Instructions from my Teachers

Chögyam Trungpa Rinpoche with the 16th Karmapa and Jamgon Kongtrul Rinpoche, Boulder, CO, circa 1974.

The Karmapa visited Boulder three times while I lived there. The first time was in 1974 by the invitation of Trungpa Rinpoche. He was hosted with great fanfare and formality. Trungpa Rinpoche told us we were welcoming a great realized being and arranged everything for us to experience his blessings.

I had the good fortune to be able to attend two Black Crown ceremonies. The story of the black crown is interesting. It is said that when the Fifth Karmapa met the Chinese Emperor Yung Lo, the emperor was able to see the Karmapa in his Sambhogakaya form as Vajradhara with the black crown above his head. The black crown is said to be the wisdom-energy form that is always above the Karmapa's head. The emperor made a physical replica of the crown so future followers of the Karmapa could receive its blessing. The crown is laden with precious stones and topped by a huge ruby. The tradition of the Black Crown Ceremony was started by the 5th Karmapa and has been given by all successive Karmapas. When the Karmapa places the black crown on his head he manifests as Avalokitesvara, the bodhisattva of compassion. He bestows a glimpse of the enlightened mind. It is said that just by seeing the black crown one will become a bodhisattva within three lifetimes. I certainly hope this is true.

I first met the 17th Karmapa in 2002. I was traveling with Ponlop Rinpoche and a group of his students. We were all escorted into a hall. This day, I think at the request of Ponlop Rinpoche, the Karmapa gave three short empowerments. One was a long-life empowerment, the other an Avalokiteshvara empowerment, and the last a guru yoga for the 16th Karmapa. After this, we were

The 16th Karmapa wearing the Black Crown.

ushered into the Karmapa's audience room.

Shortly before, I went on the pilgrimage to India with Ponlop Rinpoche. I had attended a retreat in Crestone given by Mingyur Rinpoche. During that retreat he said that if the Karmapa wanted to, he could manifest as the Sambhogakaya Buddha. I really had no idea what that meant, but when the 17th Karmapa entered the audience room I felt like someone had just beamed down from another realm. His presence was enormous and his confidence was as solid as a mountain. I felt like I was in one of those thangkas where there is this huge deity or bodhisattva and all the other beings are painted very small. This time I did not doubt that I was standing in the presence of a living Buddha.

The Karmapa took questions from the audience. I asked the Karmapa if he thought it was possible for a householder to attain enlightenment in one lifetime. He said,

> It is not something impossible. It is said that if you practice then you can accomplish liberation at home. So it is very much possible. The most important thing is exertion; your diligence is your participation in whatever you practice. Dharma practice is

Pith Instructions from my Teachers

The 17th Karmapa, Orgyen Trinley Dorje.

mainly dependent on getting the point, or not. It's nothing more or less. When you get the point you get liberation, when you don't get the point you miss it. So it is not that difficult.

The most important thing to do is to supplicate the guru and supplicate the lineage and open your heart to receive the blessings of the guru and the blessings of the lineage. Once you have those blessings then attainment of enlightenment in this life is not really a difficult thing.[1]

---

1 Personal notes from audience with Karmapa during Ponlop Rinpoche's sangha pilgrimage in 2002.

Gyuto Monastery, Sidhbari, Himachal Pradesh, India.

For many years the 17th Karmapa was essentially a prisoner of the Indian government at Gyuto Monastery. He needed to receive permission every time he wanted to travel to give teachings in India. He wasn't allowed to leave the country. In 2008, finally given permission to leave India, the Karmapa undertook his first overseas trip: an 18-day tour of Seattle, New York, Boulder, Colorado, and a short visit to California.

This first tour of the U.S. was primarily hosted by Ponlop Rinpoche and his sangha, but many other sanghas participated. There were many volunteers from the Shambhala communities and also Dzigar Kongtrul Rinpoche's students were very active and involved with the visit. I was asked to be the principal photographer for this tour.

After his 14-hour flight from New Delhi we greeted the Karmapa at the Newark airport. From the airport the Karmapa went straight to the New York Shambhala Center.

Here, at 5:00 AM the Karmapa was greeted by former students of Trungpa Rinpoche and the sanghas of Sakyong Mipham Rinpoche, Ponlop Rinpoche and others. As Karmapa climbed the steps of the large throne he joked about getting dizzy. A long mandala offering was given. This was followed by many kata offerings, including an offering from Lady Diana Mukpo, Chögyam Trungpa's wife. Karmapa then gave a brief talk. "This is my first time coming to America and I have to say I am delighted. Last night I thought I was in India and this morning I found myself in

America. Unless I look at you I find this hard to believe. I'm a little bit in a state of shock."[2]

He thanked the previous Karmapa and Trungpa Rinpoche for making everything possible. We then drove as a caravan to the hotel where the Karmapa was staying.

On Friday May 16, Karmapa began a sightseeing tour of New York City. He started with a private tour of the Metropolitan Museum on the eastern edge of Central Park. It was quite a thrill to enter the MET from a side entrance before it was open to the public. Here, in the company of the assistant curator Kurt Behrendt, we explored the museum. The Karmapa is almost always surrounded by guards. At one point in a small alcove with a painting one of the guards pulled me back. There were many occasions where I missed some precious moments with the camera lens because guards were in the way or preventing closer access.

From the MET we traveled to Ground Zero. Looking out at where the World Trade Center had once stood, Karmapa prayed for the victims of September 11, 2001.

Dzogchen Ponlop Rinpoche with HH Karmapa 17. Ground Zero, New York City, NY, 2008.

After "ground zero" we stopped at the Latse Contemporary Tibetan Cultural Library, a center of Tibetan learning and culture

---

2 Personal notes from teaching by the 17th Karmapa, New York Shambhala Center, 2008.

in New York City. The Karmapa is an aficionado of books and enjoyed browsing through their great collection.

Our last stop that day was the Rubin Museum. The Rubin houses one of the most extensive collections of Tibetan art in the world. Karmapa wanted to see a particular thangka painted in the Karma Gadri style of the 9th century.[3]

Karmapa toured the Rubin in the company of its co-founder Donald Rubin and the famed Tibetologist Eugene Smith.

The teachings the Karmapa gave in New York city were held in the Grand Ballroom at the Waldorf Astoria Hotel. His Holiness gave practical advice about how to transcend the accouterments that have come to be associated with meditation practice in the west. Rather than getting caught up in the paraphernalia of Tibetan culture, what was important was to allow one's mind to relax and rest in a natural and uncontrived wakeful way.

From New York we traveled to my hometown of Boulder, Colorado. In his first talk in Macky Auditorium at the University of Colorado, Karmapa spoke of what enlightenment means. "Rather than thinking of enlightenment as something way off in the distance, the domain of future lives, we could rather think of how enlightenment could apply to our present lifetime."[4] He went on to speak about how suffering is related to the choices we make and how we deal with our hardships—that by shifting our focus we can change our relationship to suffering.

During his tour of America, the Karmapa dedicated a lot of time addressing our current environmental issues and healing the world. In Colorado he spoke about how we cannot just assume the planet will always be here and how we needed to change our relationship to technological developments for the sake of protecting the planet.

Karmapa spoke about the need to bring our compassion out into the world. He said, "If we allow our compassion to remain only inside of ourselves our compassion will become powerless, without a function. It would become like a vase, despite having

---

3   Karma Gadri is one of the major styles of of Tibetan thangka painting. It evolved out of the Great Encampment of the Karmapa.

4   Personal notes from HH 17th Karmapa teaching at Macky Auditorium, University of Colorado, May 2008.

HH 17th Karmapa in Boulder, CO, May 2008.

the ability to carry water it had been placed high up on a shelf and never used." He went on to speak about using our imagination to generate compassion: "when the wind blows I imagine that my compassion mixes with the wind and is carried in every direction to touch all sentient beings."[5] Before leaving Boulder Karmapa visited the Boulder Shambhala Center and Naropa University.

The Karmapa gave public teachings at the Paramount Theatre in Seattle, Washington on 1 June, 2008. Although the Karmapa offered all his Seattle-area teachings in Tibetan, translated by Nalanda West's Tyler Dewar, his command of English seemed impressive. He rarely requested Tibetan translations before responding to questions posed in English. Besides the teachings the Karmapa gave at Nalanda West and the Paramount he gave a Green Tara empowerment. He ascended the throne positioned next to a shrine and beneath 20-foot with images of Green Tara and White Tara. At one point during the abhisheka, playing the bell and damaru drum, he donned the red ritual hat of the Karmapas. He also gave a long-life empowerment. At the end of the program Karmapa offered an aspiration prayer.

---

5   Personal notes from HH 17th Karmapa talks in Boulder, Colorado, May 2008.

I aspire that I become a part of you, and whatever I am becomes a part of benefiting others and the world. I don't fear losing myself anymore. I want whatever is a part of me to be a part of everyone else. My body will return to India, but my mind will stay with you. My parting aspiration for you is that you will receive a part of me and know that we will never be apart.[6]

The 17th Karmapa on a boat tour, Seattle, WA, 2008.

During his stay in Seattle the Karmapa visited the space needle and the Aerospace Museum. The highlight of my trip accompanying the retinue as a photographer was our boat tour. Mark Elliot was filming the trip while I was taking stills. At one point the Karmapa entered the steering room of the boat. He was very playful with the captain. He put on his hat and saluted.

Later during the tour I found myself in the back of the boat and I mentioned to him that we had one thing in common. Both our birthdays were on June 26. He told me that was the day everyone celebrated his birthday but that his actual birth was on June 19th. He then asked for one of my cameras and took a picture of me. I think it was Greg Conlee who took the picture below and sent it to me.

---

6 Personal notes from 17th Karmapa public teachings at the Paramount Theatre in Seattle, Washington on 1 June, 2008.

The 17th Karmapa behind the lens, taking a picture of the author, Seattle, WA, 2008.

A few years after the Karmapa US tour I decided to make a documentary on the Karmapa. This was going to be my first real venture into film. I decided I would need some professional help so I called my friend Fernanda Rivero who had a film company in Mexico City and asked her if she would be interested in working with me. She was enthusiastic and we agreed to meet in Bodhgaya.

In 2001, I met Fernanda in Delhi. Together we flew to Varanasi. After a few days enjoying the City of Lights along the ghats we went to Bodhgaya. Karmapa had staged an elaborate scene for the Kagyu Monlon on the grounds of Mingyur Rinpoche's Tergar Monastery. Fernanda and I stayed at a guest house not far from the monastery.

On the top floor of Tergar Monastery, His Holiness, the 17th Karmapa held audiences. It seemed there were no gaps in his schedule and constant meetings with long lines of those seeking his blessing. Group after group of Taiwanese, Americans, Europeans, Russians, Mexicans and the newly arrived from Tibet came to see His Holiness.

HH Karmapa blessing Tenga Rinpoche in Bodgaya during the Kagyu Monlom, 2009.

The Tibetans bowed the lowest with katas in their hands, offering precious objects they had carried for him to bless. With tears in their eyes, they would push their grandmother or sick son towards Karmapa with faith that he would heal their illnesses. No matter how long the line, he would stop occasionally to listen to their stories and then touch or blow on them before his guards hurried them past.

The Karmapa does not fit the notion we may have of a still and peaceful Buddha. On the public stage he presents a calm demeanor but in the privacy of his audience room his huge presence can barely contain itself. He often paces like a caged tiger, full of energy that does not seem to have the sufficient space to manifest. During our filming in India the Karmapa's eyes reflected little joy. He almost never smiled like he did when he toured America.

During the Monlam the Karmapa taught on the *Lamp of Atisha*. For the first two days of his teaching the Karmapa barely touched on the text itself. He spoke about the need for compassionate action. He said, that practice in the monasteries and practice on our cushions in our nice shrine rooms with all the ritual objects of Tibetan Buddhism, our drums and bells, our special bone horns and our precious malas is not good enough and is not the main point. He referred to the suffering of all beings, not just humans. He told stories about the suffering we have caused animals, from chickens in cages, animals being led to slaughter so that we can eat their meat, dogs suffering on the streets, etc. He spoke about how much suffering we have caused other beings from our actions through countless lifetimes. Even if we are not killing animals directly with our own hands we cause suffering indirectly by being the recipients and creating the demand for animal meat that others have slaughtered.

During one of our filmed interviews Karmapa said of himself, "What I really like to do is to go into action. When I am meditating on compassion I don't want to have compassion that I keep inside myself but I want to be able to show the power of compassion to others." This is one of the roles of a Karmapa.[7]

On his last day, when he had finished circumambulating the Mahabodhi Temple he offered his aspiration for the world in front of the golden Buddha statue.

In 2014, I received emails from Horst-Günter Rauprich (Vice President of Karmapa Foundation, Europe) and Stephan Kulle (a German journalist and one of the principle organizers of Karmapa's European tour) asking if I would come to Germany to photograph Karmapa's first European tour. They had seen the work I had done during Karmapa's US tour and I think my cover photo on his book The Heart is Noble. I had already given my permission for them to use my photographs to publicize the tour. I flew to Frankfurt where I was picked up at the airport and taken to Kamalashila, Karmapa's seat in Germany.

Here Karmapa gave Dharma teachings and conferred empowerments. Throughout his tour of Germany, the Karmapa spoke a great deal about the environmental crisis the world is currently facing. He said the Tibetan issue itself is not merely a political issue but an environmental issue that concerns the whole world.

> The glaciers and ice cover of the Himalayas and the Tibetan plateau serve as the source of so many of Asia's rivers that the Tibetan plateau is known as Asia's water tower. Scientists have begun referring to it as the world's Third Pole for this same reason. It is in Tibet in particular that a great many of Asia's

---

7   Personal notes from filmed interview at the Kagyu Monlom, 2009, 17th Karmapa at the Kagyu Monlom, Bodhgaya, India, 2009.

Poster photo by James Gritz, 2014.

major rivers have their point of origin, which makes the Tibetan plateau a crucial life-giving force for the natural environment of the planet generally and Asia in particular.[8]

The Karmapa emphasizes protecting the environment in his teachings. During his tours in both the US and Germany and teachings I have attended in Bodhgaya he often spoke of the need to engage in environmental action to protect the planet. *"The environmental*

---

8   Karmapa Foundation Europe. "Nurturing Compassion," November 9, 2015. https://karmapafoundation.eu/kfe-publications/nurturing-compassion/

My photograph of HH 17th Karmapa gracing the cover of his book.

emergency that we face is not just a scientific issue, nor is it just a political issue," he said. *"It is also a moral issue."*

In 2009 he created *Khoryug*, an association encouraging Tibetan Buddhist monasteries to promote environmental action in their communities. He is equally concerned with the suffering to animals and the environment by the factory farming. He made it a rule that meat is not eaten at any of the Kagyu monasteries. He also promotes women's rights in the chauvinist Tibetan Buddhist world and beyond, calling for genuine gender justice at many of his lectures and talks. It is easy to see how Karmapa is a manifestation of Avalokiteśvara, the Bodhisattva of compassion.

In Nurburgring the Karmapa gave teachings on ngöndro, the preliminary practices. He again emphasized how we could not become good practitioners without becoming good human beings. He spoke about the value of meditating on our precious human birth and impermanence and the need to cherish every moment

HH 17th Karmapa, active for environmental projects, planting a tree at Karmalashila, Germany, 2008.

of our lives. During the next few days Karmapa went on to speak about guru yoga and the importance of the lama's compassion and the disciple's devotion. Karmapa later taught on samatha, vipassana, and Mahamudra. During one of his talks he offered this story:

> Someone once asked the Third Karmapa, Rangjung Dorje, whether he had any instructions that would allow a person to become enlightened without having to meditate. "If you have any," this man said, "please give me them." In one way, this is a stupid question, and shows great arrogance, thinking you can reach enlightenment without meditating. But Rangjung Dorje told him,
> Yes, I do. But if I give it to you, it won't help you, because no matter how much I tell you not to meditate, you will try to cultivate something and will be meditating. No matter how much I tell you to leave your mind unaltered in its natural state—not to force anything but just relax—you will be altering your mind trying to reach that state. So these instructions won't help you.[9]

---

9 Personal notes from teachings by by HH Karmapa, Nürburgring, Germany, 2009.

Even though we can say of Mahamudra meditation that there is no need to meditate and nothing to alter, we cannot understand this, because we are always looking to do something. This is the problem. We all know that the human mind is what we sometimes call a monkey mind. It is so restless that we are accustomed to being disturbed and are always analyzing or engaging mentally with something or other. This is why, even if our teacher tells us, "With this practice, you do not need to do anything. Just relax and be with yourself," still we do not relax. Our minds are never at ease.

The Karmapa also gave the empowerments of 84 mahasiddhas, Medicine Buddha, Vajrasattva and Karma Pakshi, and the Second Karmapa while he was in Nurburgring. Karmapa explained how the mahasiddha Karma Pakshi was unique in the Karmapa lineage. Not only was he the first to bear the name Karmapa but he was also unique in being a holder of the secret Nyingmapa lineage. "In this way, he was someone who engaged in the unified practice of Dzogchen and Mahamudra, and the older and later tantras."[10] Karmapa said the drum he was using for the Karma Pakshi empowerment was said to have belonged to Jamyang Khyentse Chökyi Lodrö.

One of my highlights as a photographer was a visit to the legendary Grand Prix Nürburgring racetrack with Karmapa that was just across the parking lot from where the teachings were being held. Here away from the shrine halls and abhishekas there were

HH Karmapa at the Grand Prix racetrack, Nürburgring, Germany, 2009.

---

10   Ibid.

opportunities to capture some special moments. At times His Holiness likes to clown around.

In Berlin, the Karmapa's teachings were given to a sold-out crowd at the Estrel Convention Centre in Sonnenallee. The teachings were titled "Ancient Wisdom for a Modern World: Heart Advice for a Meaningful Life." Karmapa began by saying he had wanted to visit Europe since he met his first Europeans at the age of seven. He spoke about his life in Tibet and what it means to be Karmapa. He said he did not choose to be the Karmapa but as the karmapa he has given up any notion of a personal life.

> Karmapa means someone, any woman or man, who engages in the activity of a buddha. The name Karmapa itself contains the word karma, which means action in Sanskrit, the ancient language of India. The 'pa' comes from Tibetan and refers to a person. Ideally, a Karmapa is a person of action. At the other end of the spectrum, the Karmapa is a laborer, a kind of servant. The essence of the life of a Karmapa is to work or act to benefit others. If I am able to benefit others, my life as Karmapa becomes meaningful. If I am not able to benefit others, my life as Karmapa is a failure. Therefore my personal life or my life as Karmapa is oriented towards benefitting others. My responsibility—or my life as a Karmapa—is to work to benefit others, based on the Buddha's love and wisdom, lessening and eliminating the suffering of beings and increasing their happiness.[11]

He went on to say that for our lives to have meaning we must have a purpose, that our lives are interconnected and a meaningful life depends on going beyond our self-concerns and caring for others. He shared more stories from his life and spoke about loving kindness and the need to train ourselves to expand this to everyone.

---

11   Karmapa Foundation Europe. "Nurturing Compassion," November 9, 2015. https://karmapafoundation.eu/kfe-publications/nurturing-compassion/

> These beings need you. They are waiting for you. Yet since you are stuck in this prison of selfishness, you cannot extend yourself out to them. Therefore it is your responsibility, for the sake of those you feel love for, to generate strong compassion and—drawing on the strength it gives you—break out of the prison of selfishness.[12]

Again he spoke about how materialism, human greed, and desire was leading to the destruction of the environment. During the talks in Berlin the Karmapa also answered questions from a group of young people.

Boat tour of the River Spree, Berlin, Germany, 2009.

During our stay in Berlin we went on a boat tour on the River Spree. At one point during the boat tour Mark Elliot asked the Karmapa if he would take a group picture with his film crew. I was ready to take the picture when Karmapa asked me to join the group and asked someone else to take the photograph. Just before the picture was taken His Holiness whispered to me "drop all depression with the next picture." This was strange because at the time and during the European tour I had not felt depressed. However, for the last ten years I had experienced bouts of severe depression. About a year after the German tour I spent six months

---

12   Ibid.

in the deepest depression I had ever experienced. I am not sure if I will ever know if the Karmapa was referring to the past or what was to come or why he mentioned depression the moment before the picture was taken on the boat.

The 17th Karmapa praying at the Holocaust Memorial, Berlin, Germany, 2009.

After the boat tour we followed Karmapa to the Holocaust Memorial—a memorial to the Jews murdered during the Second World War. I was impressed with the size and unique design of the site. The 4.7-acre memorial is filled with concrete slabs arranged in a grid pattern and holds the names of approximately three million victims. The site was designed by the architect Peter Eisenma. After spending some time walking through the monument the Karmapa stopped to pray.

During his tour of Germany Karmapa was keen to meet with representatives from other religious traditions. During his visit in Berlin the Karmapa visited a famous synagogue and met with Rabbis Ben-Chorin and Gesa Ederberg. He partook in a special service and was asked to come up on the Bimah and view the Torah.

Near Eifel we visited the Benedictine Maria Laach Monastery where Karmapa participated with the Benedictine monks for the vespers service. On our way to Berlin Karmapa made a stop in Cologne where we toured the Cologne Cathedral in the company of the head of the archdiocese.

The 17th Karmapa at Neue Synagogue,
Berlin, Germany, 2009.

Monk pointing to statue at
Benedictine Maria Laach Monastery,
Glees, Germany, 2009.
On the 17th Karmapa's left is Ringu Tulku.

On my last day in Germany, during a fundraiser I was photographing, I said goodbye to the Karmapa. Just before I was leaving the room he said wait a minute. He handed me a signed copy of a print of his painting of Guru Rinpoche and said, "see you next time."

Print of a painting by HH Karmapa depicting Guru Rinpoche.

Mingyur Rinpoche

Yongey Mingyur Rinpoche

Besides my four principle teachers, I have also received many teachings from Yongey Mingyur Rinpoche. I met Mingyjur Rinpoche in the summer of 2002 at a retreat he was giving in Crestone, Colorado on Mahamudra and Dzogchen. He was teaching at the behest of his brother Tsoknyi Rinpoche who was occupied with responsibilities in India or Nepal. Like his brother

Tsoknyi Rinpoche, Mingyur Rinpoche draws a lot from the teachings of his father Tulku Urgyen Rinpoche and also from Nyoshul Khen Rinpoche.

I am not sure if this retreat required a prerequisite of previous retreats. I don't believe so as he gave the pointing out instructions at this retreat and that is the usual requirement for more advanced teachings. I think I can share a little from these teachings but since my notes are rather scattered I will paraphrase some of what he taught. I do remember at one point he told us to stop taking notes and just watch him teach.

Mahamudra and Dzogchen are essentially the same though the approach and some of the vocabulary is different. For instance, in Mahamudra the essence of mind is referred to as ordinary mind which I have mentioned before. In Dzogchen it is referred to as self-arising rigpa. Rinpoche laid out three stages. First, tranquility comes from the practice of samatha meditation. Second is the practice of emptiness and third is the practice of mind essence. In the ultimate stage in the Mahamudra system there is the yoga of one-pointedness and in Dzogchen the culmination of Rigpa. He also explained the seven-point posture of Vairocana.

1. Sit with the legs in lotus posture or simply crossed. If you can't do that it is alright to sit in a chair.
2. The hands are resting on the lap, right over left. You can see this in many of the statues of Buddha. You can also rest you hands on top of the knees.
3. Arms have some empty space between them like the wings of a vulture.
4. The spine is completely straight but relaxed. All teachers consider this the most important part.
5. There is a slightly downward tilt of the head.
6. Your mouth is slightly open. You are breathing through the mouth and it is best that the outbreath is longer than the inbreath. The tip of the tongue is resting on the palette.
7. The eyes are open. Having the five senses open is important to the practice. The gaze is straight

ahead and slightly up or your gaze can be at the tip of the nose or shifting our gaze from time to time.

The mind must rest naturally. The further we go from the natural state of mind, the more we increase conflicting emotions and the more fears and suffering we produce. Regarding undistracted non-meditation, the mind is generally in the present moment; when we are distracted conflicting emotions and thoughts arise. Mind essence is free from grasping, open and carefree. We are never separated from it, it's just that we don't recognize it. It is for this reason that we don't need to meditate, it is always there. We just need to recognize. Whatever arises, just let it be.[1]

Mingyur Rinpoche went on to say that sometimes you must break the meditation when practicing shamatha or rigpa. If your meditation reaches an intense experience or crescendo you have to break it. You can do this by compassion or by other means. Tsoknyi Rinpoche has talked about breaking meditation by shouting AH or dropping your hands to your legs. He went on to explain the 3 cleansing breaths, clearing the state air. I will not get into those details. You can find that on the internet. Many teachers have slightly different versions of this practice. When practicing shamatha with form or object, shamatha with sound or smell or taste or feeling, the point is to rest in a state of joy and relaxation.

In this retreat Rinpoche went on to talk about the three kayas or dream practice. He said that you could condense all practices into five main practices—Refuge, Bodhicitta, Guru Yoga, the practice on mind nature and then dedication and aspiration. He went on to cover Mahamudra and Dzogchen in detail which I will not get into in this book. I suggest if you want to explore this more you start attending some of Rinpoche's teachings on "Joy of Living" and "The Path of Liberation." There is an abundance of teachings on the Tergar website learning.tergar.org. *The Joy of Living* (2007) is also the title of his first book.

Mingyur Rinpoche has a very clear and fresh way of presenting the Dharma and presents the path in a very organized fashion.

---

1   Personal notes from Mingyur Rinpoche teachings in Crestone, Colorado, circa 2002.

In level one Rinpoche introduces the student to the practice of open awareness, the discovery of who we truly are. Understanding that all phenomena are impermanent and interdependent one begins to see that the world is our own projection or construction. Level 2 is also about opening the heart of love and compassion. Level 3 is called "awakening wisdom." In level 3 we are introduced to the practice of analytic meditation which helps us undo our constructed and false view of reality. With the investigation of analytic meditation we can unravel our assumptions about life leading us to a joyful life and open heart.

Rinpoche's follow up courses are called "The Path of Liberation" which includes "the Nectar of the Path Course." All these teachings are available in great detail, including talks, readings, and guided meditations from learning.tergar.org Teachings on nature of mind, Mahamudra and Dzogchen are also presented. Most of these have the prerequisite of completing the "Joy of Living" series.

During the time I was filming the documentary of HH 17th Karmapa in June of 2011, I attended teachings of Mingyur Rinpoche in Bodhgaya. The continuing thread during these teachings was working with the mind and relaxing into open awareness. During these teachings he said, "Taking fruition as the path is the essence of Vajrayana practice." I think he meant realizing the nature of mind, knowing you already have Buddha nature and recognizing this is our path.

Mingyur Rinpoche, Bodhgaya, 2011.

I had an interview with Rinpoche on the last night of his teachings in Bodhgaya. I was having a nyam experience brought on by some of his teachings on awareness and the various types of meditation. The one that penetrated the most was what Rinpoche called river meditation. In river meditation, one is not simply being aware of just one object like the breath or a statue like in samatha with form. In river meditation one lets the awareness move toward whatever arises. There is an awareness of being alive with all senses open. Listening to the birds, the sound of traffic, voices on the street, someone coughing nearby, the smell of incense, a door slamming closed, the slight pain in your lower back and neck, the sense of feeling your skin touching the air, the random thoughts arising in your mind. Mingyur Rinpoche describes the river experience in *Joy of Living*: "Gradually as you continue to practice, you'll inevitably find yourself able to clearly distinguish the movements of thoughts, emotions, and sensations through your mind ... things are still moving, but more slowly and gently."[2]

Walking to Mingyur Rinpoche's quarters I found myself in a state of open clarity. My thoughts arose slowly and clearly with more space in-between each one. All my senses were sharp and I felt at ease as I walked into his living room. I can't even remember if we talked or just sat there together. I think Rinpoche might have reminded me to not get hung up on temporary experiences. Unexpectedly, Tsoknyi Rinpoche walked into the room. He said, "Ah you are here" and he left the room.

The next day after his teachings in Bodhgaya were finished, Mingyur Rinpoche left his monastery to begin an extended retreat. He departed in the middle of the night without telling anyone. He did not take any money or belongings, just the clothes he was wearing. Mingyur Rinpoche wrote this letter to his students around the world shortly before he left for retreat.

> Dear friends, students, and fellow meditators,
>
> By the time you read this letter, I will have begun the long retreat that I announced last year. As you may

---

[2] Yongey Mingyur, and Eric Swanson. *The Joy of Living: Unlocking the Secret and Science of Happiness*. New York, NY: Harmony/Rodale, 2008, p, 215.

know, I have felt a very strong connection with the tradition of retreat since I was a young boy growing up in the Himalayas. Even though I didn't really know how to meditate, I would often run away from home to a cave nearby, where I would sit quietly and chant the mantra "om mani padma hung" over and over again in my mind. My love of the mountains and the simple life of a wandering meditator called to me even then.

It wasn't until I was in my early teens that I got my first chance to do a formal retreat. Until that time, I lived at Nagi Gompa, a small hermitage on the outskirts of Kathmandu. It was there that my father, Tulku Urgyen Rinpoche, first taught me how to meditate. After training with him for a number of years, I heard that a traditional three-year retreat was scheduled to begin at Sherab Ling, Kenting Tai Situ Rinpoche's monastery in India.

Though I was still only eleven years old, I begged my father to let me go. He was happy to see my enthusiasm since he himself had stayed in retreat for more than twenty years over the course of his life. When we talked about the idea of me going into a strict, traditional retreat, he told me about the great yogi Milarepa and how important his example has been to generations of Tibetan Buddhist meditators.

Milarepa's early life was filled with misery and hardship. Despite all the bad karma he created as a young man, he eventually overcame his dark past and attained complete enlightenment while living in isolated caves deep in the mountains. Once he was enlightened, Milarepa thought that there was no longer any need for him to stay in the mountains. He made up his mind to go down to more populated areas where he could directly help alleviate the suffering of others. One night, not too long after he decided to depart, Milarepa had a dream about his teacher Marpa. In the dream, Marpa encouraged him to stay in retreat, telling him that through his example he would touch the lives of countless people.

After telling me about Milarepa's remarkable life, my father said, "Marpa's prophecy came to pass. Even though Milarepa spent most of his life living in remote caves, millions of people have been inspired by his example over the centuries. By demonstrating the importance of practicing in retreat, he influenced the entire tradition of Tibetan Buddhism. Thousands and thousands of meditators have manifested the qualities of enlightenment because of his dedication.

A few years later, during my first three-year retreat, I had the good fortune to study with another great master, Saljey Rinpoche. In the middle of the third year, I and a few of my fellow retreatants approached Rinpoche to ask his advice. We had derived tremendous benefit from the retreat and asked him how we could help uphold this precious lineage. "Practice!" Saljey Rinpoche responded, "I've been in retreat almost half my life. This is a genuine way to help others. If you want to preserve the lineage, transform your minds. You won't find the true lineage anywhere else."

The teachings and example of both my father and Saljey Rinpoche deeply inspired me. This inspiration, coupled with my own natural desire to practice in retreat, has been a guiding light throughout my life.

When my first formal retreat ended, Saljey Rinpoche passed away and Tai Situ Rinpoche asked me to take his place as retreat master. I accepted my new role and have now been leading retreats and teaching meditation for twenty years. In particular, in the last ten years, I have spent a great deal of time teaching around the world. I've been to more than thirty countries, sharing my experience of overcoming the panic attacks I experienced as a child and passing on the teachings that my masters entrusted to me. Over the years, I've come to see the truth of the words of my father and Saljey Rinpoche. As they both taught me, the experience gained in retreat can be a powerful tool in helping others.

In my early years, I trained in a number of different ways. The time I spent with my father involved rigorous meditation training, but I was not in strict retreat, in the sense that I met other people and could come and go freely. My three-year retreat at Sherab Ling Monastery, on the other hand, was held in complete isolation. A small group of us lived in an enclosed compound and didn't have any contact with the outside world until the retreat ended. These are two forms of practice, but they are not the only ways. As demonstrated by the great yogi Milarepa, there is also a tradition of wandering from place to place, staying in remote caves and sacred sites with no plans or fixed agenda, just an unswerving commitment to the path of awakening. This is the type of retreat that I will be practicing over the coming years.

This tradition isn't very common these days. My third main teacher, the great Dzogchen yogi Nyoshul Khen Rinpoche, was one of the few recent masters to practice in this way. Khen Rinpoche practiced in closed retreats when he was younger, but later he took up the life of a wandering yogi. He completely dropped his normal life and activities. Nobody knew where he was or what he was doing. He spent time meditating in isolated caves and other places where the great masters of times past, such as Milarepa and Longchenpa practiced, and at one point he even lived among the Hindu sadhus of India. His story is a perfect example of a modern, carefree yogi.

More recently, Tai Situ Rinpoche, the last of my four main teachers, talked about meditating in mountain retreats during a teaching he gave in 2009. Over four months, Rinpoche passed on the lineage of an important meditation text called The Ocean of the Definitive Meaning. This is one of the main instruction manuals used by meditators in the Kagyu lineage.

I mention my teachers here because their wisdom and compassion has nurtured my desire to make retreat a focal point of my life. My father and Saljey Rinpoche encouraged and supported my first experiences in retreat, while Nyoshul Khen Rinpoche and Tai Situ Rinpoche inspired me to embark on the path of a wandering yogi. Like a tiny firefly in the midst of the sun's radiance, I can never hope to compare to my precious teachers, but without their example and inspiration, I would not have followed this path.

You might think that while I'm on retreat we won't be able to stay connected to each other. Of course, we won't be able to see each other for a few years, but don't forget that our connection is through the Dharma. It isn't simply seeing our teachers, or even hearing them, that creates a spiritual bond. It's when we take the teachings we've received and bring them into our own experience that an unshakeable connection is formed. The more we practice, the stronger the bond with our teacher becomes.

Three of my four teachers have long since passed away. At times, I remember what it was like being with them and hearing them teach. I remember how joyful and light they were, and how they carried themselves with such dignity and freedom. These memories make me a little sad, but when I remember what they taught me and let their wisdom fill my being, I can feel their presence anywhere and anytime. So while you and I may be apart physically over the next few years, through our practice we will always be together.

I feel a great sense of warmth and love when I think of all of you, like we're one big family. So don't worry, I'm not having a mid-life crisis. I'm not going on retreat because I'm sick of traveling, or sick of teaching students. In fact, it's just the opposite. During this time our practice will bring us closer.

There are times in our lives when we focus on learning and study, and others where we take what we've learned and bring it deeply into our experience.

These are processes that each of us goes through individually, but having the support of a community can be a great help as we follow the path. It has been wonderful to see how many of you have come together in recent years to help form and shape our growing community. Though I've helped support the community through my teachings, the community itself is yours. It is there to support you on the path of awakening, and it will be your commitment and support that will allow for the flourishing of the community in years to come. Receiving support and guidance from the community, and giving back in whatever way we can, is an integral part of the journey.

To help you continue along the path, I've prepared many teachings over the past few years that will be delivered by my emanations. These emanations can appear magically almost anywhere and will teach you just what you need to deepen your practice. What am I talking about? Modern technology, of course! We recorded hundreds of hours of teachings on a whole range of topics, and these teachings will be made available over the coming years. Some will be used for online courses and seminars, others will be shown at Tergar centers and groups, and some will be freely available online. In some ways, my video emanations are better than the real me. You won't have to feed them or put them up in a hotel. They will wait patiently until you're ready for them. And most importantly, they won't feel bad if you get bored and turn them off!

Don't mistakenly think that your DVD player will be your new root guru. Recorded teachings can never take the place of a direct transmission from teacher to student. What I'm trying to say is that there will still be plenty of opportunities to study and practice, especially for those of you who are following the Joy of Living and Path of Liberation programs. There are also other wonderful lamas to study with, including His Holiness Karmapa, Orgyen Trinley Dorje, and my teacher Tai Situ Rinpoche. My brother, Tsoknyi Rinpoche, is also an excellent teacher and has agreed to guide the Tergar community while I'm away. Finally, we have our own Tergar lamas and instructors who will lead retreats and workshops all over the world. In fact, there will be so much happening, you may not even notice I'm gone!

In parting, I would like to give you one small piece of advice to keep in your heart. You may have heard me say this before, but it is the key point of the entire path, so it bears repeating: All that we are looking for in life—all the happiness, contentment, and peace of mind—is right here in the present moment. Our very own awareness is itself fundamentally pure and good. The only problem is that we get so caught up in the ups and downs of life that we don't take the time to pause and notice what we already have.

Don't forget to make space in your life to recognize the richness of your basic nature, to see the purity of your being and let its innate qualities of love, compassion, and wisdom naturally emerge. Nurture this recognition as you would a small seedling. Allow it to grow and flourish.

Many of you have generously asked how you can help support my retreat. My answer is simple: Keep this teaching at the heart of your practice. Wherever you are and whatever you are doing, pause from time to time and relax your mind. You don't have to change anything about your experience. You can let thoughts and feelings come and go freely and leave your senses wide open. Make friends with your experience and see if you can notice the spacious awareness that is with you all the time. Everything you ever wanted is right here in this present moment of awareness.

I will keep you in my heart and in my prayers."

— *Yours in the Dharma, Yongey Mingyur Rinpoche*

Mingyur Rinpoche has made a commitment to teaching and leading retreats in Mexico. He has a sizable Tergar community in Puebla Mexico. I have gone to several of these retreats and I hope to continue attending his teachings.

Conclusion

Pith instructions are usually considered the most profound personal and practical teachings passed from the master to the disciple. These teaching are passed on through direct oral instructions, referred to as the ear-whispered lineage. They might take the form of a direct passing on the highest teachings like Dzogchen and Mahamudra, but I think pith instructions come in many forms. For me, the First Noble Truth from the Buddha that life is suffering is a pith instruction. Without this realization, we experience a constant flow of uneasiness or anxiety, no matter how subtle, who would even think of entering a path like Buddhism? Understanding that impermanence is the nature of all compounded things is also a pith instruction.

There are many examples of sudden and direct instruction, like Tilopa hitting Naropa with the sandal which brought his realization of the nature of mind. My favorite story is the one of Patrul Rinpoche and his disciple Nyoshul Lungtok. Nyoshul Lungtak was a very disciplined practitioner, but he had never realized the nature of mind. One night he was with Patrul Rinpoche at a hermitage above Dzogchen Monastery. He told Patrul Rinpoche he had not experienced the nature of mind. They were lying together on the ground looking up into the clear starry sky.

Patrul Rinpoche asked him, "Do you see the stars up there in the sky?"

"Yes."

"Do you hear the dogs barking in Dzogchen Monastery?"

"Yes."

"Well, that's it."

It is said you can find the awakened state in the gap between conceptual thoughts. In Mahamudra, it is called *thamal gyi shepa*, or ordinary mind. In Dzogchen, this moment of pure awareness free from the discursive mind is called rigpa. Tsoknyi Rinpoche has referred to it as baby rigpa. As this state becomes more subtle it becomes the true state of rigpa. By continuously recognizing these moments of naked awareness the view becomes refined and gains stability. Without the pointing out instructions from a guru these raw moments of wisdom are difficult to find let alone rest in.

It is said in Dzogchen and Mahamudra the true nature of mind is so close we don't recognize it. It is like looking for the sunglasses that are already on your head.

We are always searching for something glorious, lights flashing, peace, joy, nirvana. Always something outside. In both Mahamudra and Dzogchen the practice is turning in the other direction and looking inside. Vajrayana is the path of fruition. There is nothing outside to obtain, we are already primordial pure from beginningless time. The only difference between an awakened Buddha and ourselves is that we are distracted, obscured by the habitual patterns and projections that direct our lives. In Vajrayana it is said that fruition is the path. Once obscurations are removed we find the nature of mind. In Dzogchen this awakened state is often called primordial purity.

Because this flash experience of awakened mind is difficult to recognize my suggestion to anyone who does not have a teacher is that you find a genuine Vajrayana master. Someone who can point out the nature of mind so you have the chance to recognize it. Once recognized little by little you need to experience the continuity of primordial awareness. I have heard it compared to a piece of paper that has been poked by a pin. One small hole in the paper will not accomplish the continuity of awareness that is needed to move toward enlightenment. But if this paper is penetrated again and again, thousands and thousands of times eventually it falls apart. This ego-clinging, caught in the endless web of distractions and habits is hard to give up. It needs to be poked with the pin again and again. This is the job of the Vajra master, the guru who can lead you to the other side and freedom from your preconceptions and projections.

Devotion plays a big part in the tantric path. Devotion to the guru develops confidence in the path. The more confidence you have developed in the guru and the teachings of the Buddha he is transmitting the more blessings descend and the quicker you will travel to awakening.

In a talk called 'Approaching the Guru' Dzongsar Khyentse Rinpoche said that "there are many different methods for recognizing this Buddha within. Of these, the quickest and easiest is to receive the blessings of the guru. This is why guru devotion is necessary. For example, you may be having a nightmare about monsters. But then suddenly, somebody throws a bucket of cold water over you and you wake up. The cold water doesn't really make the monsters disappear, because there were no monsters in the first place. It was just a dream. But on the other hand, when you are having a nightmare, your suffering is real, and the person who throws the bucket of water over you is indeed very kind and special.

If you have a lot of merit, you are able to meet such a person, a person who can throw the water. On the other hand, if you don't have merit, you may never wake up from the nightmare."[1] If you have true devotion, everything can be taken as a manifestation of your guru.

There are obviously pros and cons to having more than one teacher. Sometimes it feels awkward to be in one of your teacher's communities when you might be the only one who feels devotion for more than their guru. Sangha members can be very territorial about their teachers, not only about trying to keep newcomers from getting too close to the teacher, but also feeling that anyone who has other teachers might not really be as devoted and loyal to their teacher. But more importantly, you see many of your fellow sangha members devoting themselves wholeheartedly to working for the mandala of their teacher and you feel uncertain as to where to put your energy or even to which sangha you should pay dues.

The deeper you and the teacher get into the Vajrayana teachings like deity yoga, sadhana practice, Dzogchen teachings, etc. the more confusing it can be to follow more than one teacher. There is no doubt in my mind that when one is dedicated to only one teacher it is much easier and simplifies your path. I often think about this.

On the other hand, there are some advantages to having more than one teacher. Sometimes I imagine that when I am dying, perhaps I would have a friend try to get a hold of one of my teachers to see if he could possibly come and help me through the process of death. With five teachers there might be more chance that one would be free or happen to be traveling nearby. I never planned on

---

1 Approaching the Guru. A talk on devotion by Dzongsar Khyentse Rinpoche, given in 1996 in Boulder, Colorado, at the commmoration of the death of His Holiness Dilgo Khyentse Rinpoche. *Lion's Roar*, November, 2000.

having more than one teacher but once you do you are stuck. There is a Samaya bond I feel with all my teachers. When you have several teachers and feel love and devotion for all of them, whom would you drop? It would be like abandoning one of your parents. Would you really abandon your father or mother just to have less confusion?

There are some other advantageous aspects of having more than one teacher. For example, not too many years ago I was listening to Dzongsar Khyentse Rinpoche giving some complex and subtle teachings. At the time I remember feeling extremely grateful for having spent so many years with Tsoknyi Rinpoche and Ponlop Rinpoche, hearing teachings on the same subject from different angles. It helped me to comprehend what Dzongsar Khyentse Rinpoche was teaching. I find this to be true when listening to all my teachers. They present the same Dharma transmitted down through an uninterrupted lineage all the way back to Sakyamuni Buddha. It is the same Dharma because it is the true Dharma and the true nature of reality. In many cases, they share many of the same teachers and lineages. In some cases, they are conveying the same cycle of teachings, having received the same empowerment, yet all of them have had their different masters and received their personal pith instructions. Teachers have varied styles and skillful means when transmitting and communicating Dharma. I find this extremely helpful for understanding the teachings.

Even though one teacher may be a strict vegetarian and another eats meat, one might drink alcohol and have girlfriends and another is married or a monk, they all present the fundamental truths of the path to enlightenment. I cannot remember one single occasion where any one of my teachers said something that was in contradiction to another's teaching. Every one of my teachers no matter how questionable some actions might appear to ordinary people has in every moment and in every word been impeccably faithful to the teachings of the Buddha. It is hard for me to imagine not having any one of my teachers as a guide on the path. I remember once Jigme Khyentse Rinpoche said to me, "All the lineage holders are available to you." Whenever I have doubts about whether I have too many teachers I think about those words.

There is a lot of talk in the Tibetan Buddhist Vajrayana scene about who is your root teacher. This used to be a question in my mind. I once asked the 17th Karmapa, Orgyen Trinley Dorje, how do you know who your root guru is? He said, "Your root guru is the one who points out the nature of your mind to you." Then I asked, what if you feel like all your gurus do that. I went on to ask, "Who do you visualize as the Deity during your sadhana practice?" He said, "You can mix them all together when you visualize the Yidam and then dissolve them all into yourself at the end."

Perhaps the most profound advice I have received from my teachers that has been passed down through the Dzogchen lineage is "short moments, many times." It is difficult to sustain rigpa, ordinary mind, the natural state, or whatever you would like to call it. It often comes out of nowhere, when you drop your practice, when you sneeze, or when you have lost awareness stepping off the curb and are almost run over by a car. These are accidental moments over which you have no control. For me, "short moments, many times" is a way to practice. Even in a longer practice session, you can take this approach. You can let go of the concept of practice you are clinging to, take a break, and rest for a brief moment. Sometimes when I find myself feeling flat I think of my gurus, their awake mind and their hearts of compassion. For me, this freshens the space of awareness. Thoughts might drop away, and I hear the birds, the hum of space free from thoughts and I can rest for a few moments. When your mind starts running after thoughts or even when your mind seems frozen in a quiet state of so-called meditation you can break your practice by shouting the Tibetan syllable *Ah* or *Phet*.

Outside of formal practice, there are so many opportunities. While your partner may be rambling on about all the difficulties she or he may have experienced with their boss that day you can rest without thought or judgment while listening. You may find yourself sitting in the doctor's office waiting impatiently for your appointment and you can let go and just rest in awareness. You can rest in awareness in your car stopped at the red light, standing in line at the ATM, or in the grocery store. There are so many occasions, so many convenient moments. How can you even have the thought "I do not have time to practice?" This is what I tell myself when I find I am caught up in confusion, conflicting thoughts, or emotions. So often the engine of our mind keeps running even after we have parked the car. Mindfulness or open awareness or even trekchö practice is not something complicated or contrived. Even the word practice is misleading because you are not trying to accomplish anything. It does involve a willingness to let go of the solidity you have created and just rest in what is.

> Training is simply short moments of recognition repeated many times and supported by devotion and compassion.[2]

The sound of the wind blowing through the trees. An owl calling in the distance. No thought of near and far. Not even the label owl exists. The sun is warm on the side of your face. The breeze gently caresses your hair. There is no distinction between your hair and the breeze. A dog is barking down the street. Sounds of construction from your neighbor's house. A bucket drops to the ground. A rooster crows. Like a river flowing your awareness takes in whatever is happening but you are not captured. There is no separation between perceiver and perceived. Just raw awareness. Continuous. Present.

If we try to remain undistracted and stay present moment to moment in our life, I think we will eventually find what we are looking for, the awakened state.

> May the teachers' lives be long.
> May the dharma flourish for as long
> as there are beings in Samsara.
> Having heard the teachings of the Buddha
> and received the blessings of the lineage,
> may all beings cross to the other shore.

---

2 Tulku Urgyen Rinpoche and Tsoknyi Rinpoche. "As the Clouds Vanish." *Tricycle: The Buddhist Review*, Winter 1999. https://tricycle.org/magazine/clouds-vanish/.

Suggested Reading

Dorje, Ogyen Trinley. *The Heart Is Noble: Changing the World from the Inside Out.* Boston, MA: Shambhala Publications, 2013.

Dowman, Keith, trans. *The Flight of the Garuda: The Dzogchen Tradition of Tibetan Buddhism.* 2nd ed. Somerville, MA: Wisdom Publications, 1994.

Khyentse, Dilgo. *Primordial Purity: Oral Instructions on the Three Words That Strike the Vital Point.* Boulder, CO: Shambhala Publications, 2016.

———. *Pure Appearance: Development and Completion Stages in Vajrayana Practice.* Boulder, CO: Shambhala Publications, 2016.

Khyentse, Dzongsar Jamyang. *Not for Happiness: A Guide to the So-Called Preliminary Practices.* Boston, MA: Shambhala Publications, 2012.

———. *The Guru Drinks Bourbon?* Boulder, CO: Shambhala Publications, 2016.

Padmasambhava. *Light of Wisdom, Volumes I-IV.* Edited by Marcia Binder Schmidt. Boudhanath, Hong Kong, and Esby: Rangjung Yeshe Publications, 2004.

Patrul, Rinpoche. *Words of My Perfect Teacher: A Complete Translation of a Classic Introduction to Tibetan Buddhism.* New Haven, CT: Yale University Press, 2011.

Ponlop, Dzogchen. *Mind Beyond Death.* Boston, MA: Shambhala Publications, 2008.

———. *Wild Awakening: The Heart of Mahamudra and Dzogchen.* Boston, MA: Shambhala Publications, 2003.

Ponlop, Rinpoche Dzogchen. *Penetrating Wisdom: The Aspiration of Samantabhadra.* Ithaca, NY: Snow Lion Publications, 2006.

Rinpoche, Yongey Mingyur, and Helen Tworkov. *In Love with the World: A Monk's Journey Through the Bardos of Living and Dying.* New York, NY: Random House Publishing Group, 2019.

Thrangu, Khenchen. *The Ninth Karmapa's Ocean of Definitive Meaning.* Boston, MA: Shambhala Publications, 2011.

Trungpa, Chögyam. *Meditation in Action.* Boston, MA: Shambhala Publications, 2010.

———. *The Collected Works of Chögyam Trungpa*. Edited by Carolyn Rose Gimian. Vol. 8. Boston, MA: Shambhala Publications, 2004.

Tsoknyi, Drubwang. *Carefree Dignity: Discourses on Training in the Nature of Mind*. Boudhanath, Hong Kong, and Esby: Rangjung Yeshe Publications, 2004.

———. *Fearless Simplicity: The Dzogchen Way of Living Freely in a Complex World*. Boudhanath, Hong Kong, and Esby: Rangjung Yeshe Publications, 2003.

Urgyen, Tulku. *As It Is*. Boudhanath, Hong Kong, and Esby: Rangjung Yeshe Publications, 1999.

Online Resources

https://learning.tergar.org
https://fullybeing.org
https://tsoknyirinpoche.org
https://siddharthasintent.org
https://www.lionsroar.com
https://dpr.info/
https://nalandabodhi.org/teacher/dzogchen-ponlop-rinpoche/
https://all-otr.org
https://shambhalaarchives.org/collections/
https://chögyamtrungpa.com
https://www.naropa.edu/academics/library/archives-and-special-collections/
https://www.chronicleproject.com
https://www.rigpawiki.org/index/php?title=Main_Page
https://tricycle.org/magazine/resource-roundup-cybersangha/
https://www.shambhala.com/online-courses/buddhist/
https://kagyutd.org
https://nitarthainstitute.org/programs/online-courses/self-paced-online-courses/
https://www.youtube.com/results?search_query=Siddhartha%27s+intent+youtube

Glossary of Buddhist Terms

Abhisheka is granting an empowerment to practice a special vajrayana deity practice. The empowerment creates a special bond between guru and disciple.

Bardo is the intermediate state or gap we experience between death and our next rebirth. Most commonly it refers to the 49 days between death and rebirth. Bardo can also refer to the gap or space we experience between any two states. There are 6 states of Bardo The bardo of birth and death, bardo of dreaming, the bardo of meditation, the bardo of the moment of death, the bardo of clear light or luminosity and the bardo of becoming.

Bodhicitta refers to the awakened mind; the state of mind of the bodhisattva and the wish to liberate all beings. It is also divided into absolute and relative bodhicitta. The absolute level is the nature of mind.

Bodhisattva is the mind of the spiritual warrior and one who has attained the realization of the 10 bodhisattva bhumis In Mahayana Buddhism, bodhisattva is one who unselfish motivation to put others before oneself, which includes forgoing enlightenment until all others have achieved it. Sometimes the example of a captain who crosses samsara leading beings to the other shore of nirvana.

Buddha Nature is a kind of seed or cause of Buddhahood. It is the potential or cause of enlightenment that exists in the mindstream of all sentient beings.

Daka is the male version of dakini and is the tantric equivalent of a Bodhisattva.

Dakini is a female enlightened practioner of tantra who protect the dharma and the practitioner. It is the femine principle connected to wisdom. Dakinis are refered to as "sky dancers" The word literally means moving through the sky.

Dharmakaya is Buddha-mind, the mind's all pervasive empty essence free from all conceptual contrivance or elaboration.

Dharma refers to the teachings of the Buddha (Skt. Buddhadharma). It has many shades of meaning, including 'the spiritual path', or 'spirituality' in general. The word can also mean phenomena.

Deity (Yidam) is an enlightened being visualized in male or female, peaceful or wrathful form. The Yidam is considered the root of accomplishment. Usually, the guru gives the yidam practice to a disciple after the prelimary practices or ngöndro.

Dzogchen is the practice of the "Great Perfection". As Yongey Mingyur Rinpoche wrote in *Lion's Roar*, "Dzogchen is treasured above all other practices in the Nyingma school of Vajrayana Buddhism because it helps us connect directly with our own enlightened nature." It is considered the highest teaching and the highest meditation practice leading to the realization of the nature of mind.

Drupchen is an intensive group practice meditation retreat. It involves a complete sadhana practice, with all the mantras, mudras, tormas and a sand mandala and usually takes place over 7 to 10 days.

Empowerment: see **Abhisheka**.

Hinayana is a lesser vehicle or path. It focuses on the direct teachings of the historic Buddha and sometimes refers to an emphasis on self-liberation rather than the Mahayana or greater vehicle's idea of liberation of all sentient beings before one's own enlightenment. It is often confused with Theravada.

Karma literally means action, but refers to the concept that all intentions and actions have consequences, whether they are positive or negative. All actions sooner or later come to fruition whether in this of future lifetimes.

Karuna means compassion, sympathy, or mercy for others. The special kindness shown to those who suffer.

Kleshas is a Sanskrit word referring to "defilements." These are deluded states of mind or emotions that lead to suffering. The six root kleshas are ignorance, desire, pride, anger, doubt and wrong views.

Luminosity in the Vajrayana Buddhist context is radiance or clarity, the union of appearance and emptiness.

Maha Ati is one sub-division of the nine yanas taught by the Nyingma school of Tibetan Buddhism.

Mahamudra literally means 'Great Seal' referring to the seal of ultimate reality. It is a meditation path leading to the direct realization of the nature of mind. If seriously interested one could study the renowned book *Mahamudra, The Ocean of Definitive Meaning* by The Ninth Gyalwang Karmapa and Wangchuk Dorje, Nithartha International, 2001. The free pdf can be accessed here: https://archive.org/details/mahamudra-ocean-of-definitive-meaning-wangchuk-dorje-copy-3

Mahayana or Great Vehicle is a later philosophical and sectarian development in Buddhism that typically emphasizes the compassion and wisdom ideal of the bodhisattva. In Mahayana Buddhism the goal is liberation for all sentient beings, rather than liberation for individuals. The path of Mahayana emphasizes compassion and the realization of the emptiness of self and other.

Madhyamika or "The Middle Way" or "doctrine of emptiness" was founded by Nagarjuna, a scholar of Nalanda University and teaches the absence of any true existence or non-existence of reality. Excellent teachings on Madhyamika can be found from Dzongsar Khyentse in *Introduction to the Middle Way: Chandrakirti's Madhyamakavatara with Commentary by Dzongsar Jamyang Khyentse Rinpoche*. Dordogne, France: Khyentse Foundation, © 1996, p. 8. The pdf is free and you can find it here: http://dzongsarinstitute.org.in/en/wp-content/uploads/2018/03/Introduction-to-the-Middle-Way-by-DJKR.pdf There is also an excellent article by Dzogchen Ponlop Rinpoche that can be found here: https://www.lionsroar.com/through-the-lens-of-madhyamaka/

Mantra is a series of syllables (often, but not always, Sanskrit) meant to be recited as part of visualization practice that can protect the mind of the practitioner.

Nirvana means "blown out" as in an oil lamp, to pass beyond suffering. It is the goal of the Buddhist path, and in English is translated as enlightenment or complete awakening.

Ngöndro refers to the preliminary, preparatory or foundational practices or disciplines common to all four schools of Tibetan Buddhism.vUsually precedes deity yoga. Four times

100,000 refuge and bodhicitta, Vajrasattva, mandala offering, and guru yoga.

Padmasambhava or (Lotus born) also known as **Guru Rinpoche** (Precious Guru) and the **Lotus from Oḍḍiyāna**, was a tantric Buddhist master from India who brought Vajrayana to Tibet. Padmasambhava was said to reside on the peak of the Copper Colored Mountain.

Puja is a ceremony in which offerings and other acts of devotion and prayer are performed.

Rigpa as it relates to Dzogchen teachings means knowing the nature of the mind, pure awareness.

Sadhana literally 'means of accomplishment'. A sadhana is a ritual text presenting the means to accomplish one or several deities, who in essence are the ultimate state of a Buddha.

Samaya is the vajrayana commitment taken during Abhishekas that creates a bond between the student and the teacher. Jamgong Kongtrul says, Samanya is the manner in which the student can "preserve the life-force of that empowerment within your being."

Samsara is the cyclic existence that beings are trapped in, comprised of birth-life-suffering-sickness-death-rebirth and caused by ignorance.

Sangha is a community that practices the dharma together. It's one of the Three Jewels in which Buddhists take refuge, along with the Buddha and the dharma.

Samatha means 'calm abiding' and is also translated as 'peacefully remaining' or 'tranquillity meditation'.

Sunyata or emptiness is the absence of inherent existence in all phenomena, the true nature of all phenomena.

Six Realms refers to the six earthly realms of the gods, *asuras* (anti-gods), humans, animals, *pretas* (hungry ghosts), and *narakas* (hell realms).

Skandha literally means "piled up" or "heaps". The five skandhas are form, feeling, perceptions, mental formation and consciousness.

Three Yanas refers to the 'three vehicles' or schools of thought that developed from the Buddha's teaching: Hinayana, Mahayana and Vajrayana.

Tonglen is the practice of exchanging oneself for others. One takes on the suffering and pain of others, and give them your happiness, and well-being.

Upadesha is a teaching or instruction. It is the spiritual guidance provided by a guru or spiritual teacher.

Vajrayana or 'Vajra Vehicle'. also called the secret mantra or mantrayana. The Vajrayana is a path based on cultivating pure perception. It is considered the path to swiftly attain a direct realization of buddha nature and the nature of reality itself.

Vipashyana is 'clear seeing' or meditation that develops insight into the nature of reality. It is one of the two main aspects of the practice of meditation on the Buddhist path, the other being shamatha, or 'calm abiding'.

Yana means "vehicle" to enlightenment, as in Buddhism's three yanas: the of yana of individual liberation, the Mahayana, and the Vajrayana.

Bibliography

Dowman, Keith, trans. *The Flight of the Garuda: The Dzogchen Tradition of Tibetan Buddhism*. 2nd ed. Somerville, MA: Wisdom Publications, 1994.

Elliott, Mark. "What Trungpa Rinpoche Accomplished: Khyentse Yangsi Rinpoche Reflects on Chogyam Trungpa Rinpoche's Life and Teachings." The Chronicles of Chögyam Trungpa Rinpoche, March 21, 2018. https://www.chronicleproject.com/what-trungpa-rinpoche-did/.

Facebook. "Dzongsar Jamyang Khyentse Facebook Page," n.d. https://www.facebook.com/djkhyentse.

Gampopa, and Khenpo Karthar Rinpoche. *The Instructions of Gampopa: A Precious Garland of the Supreme Path (Dream Flag Series)*. Translated by Lama Yeshe Gyamtso. Ithaca, NY: Snow Lion Publications, 1996.

Gritz, James, and Maria Fernanda Rivero. *Never Give Up: The Heart of Compassion*. India, 2011.

Gurdjieff, George Ivanovich. *Meetings With Remarkable Men*. New York, NY: E.P. Dutton & Company, Inc., 1969.

Hayward, Jeremy. *Warrior-King of Shambhala: Remembering Chogyam Trungpa*. Somerville, MA: Wisdom Publications, 2007.

Karmapa Foundation Europe. "Nurturing Compassion," November 9, 2015. https://karmapafoundation.eu/kfe-publications/nurturing-compassion/.

Khyentse, Dilgo. *Primordial Purity: Oral Instructions on the Three Words That Strike the Vital Point*. Boulder, CO: Shambhala Publications, 2016.

Khyentse, Dzongsar. "The Path of Guru Devotion." The Chronicles of Chögyam Trungpa Rinpoche, April 11, 2019. https://www.chronicleproject.com/dzongsar-khyentse-rinpoche-2/#:~:text=Ch%C3%B6gyam%20Trungpa%20Rinpoche%20was%20a,and%20finally%20stirring%20things%20up.

Khyentse, Dzongsar Jamyang. *The Guru Drinks Bourbon?* Boulder, CO: Shambhala Publications, 2016.

Kunsang, Erik Pema. "Fortress Peak, the Cover Picture." *Blazing-

Splendor (blog), August 11, 2005. http://blazing-splendor.blogspot.com/2005/08/fortress-peak-cover-picture.html.

———. "Samten Gyatso's Transmission of the New Treasures." *Blazing-Splendor* (blog), April 8, 2009. http://blazing-splendor.blogspot.com/2009/04/?m=1.

Padmasambhava. *The Light of Wisdom.* Translated by Erik Pema Kunsang. Vol. 1. Boudhanath, Hong Kong, and Esby: Rangjung Yeshe Publications, 1999.

Ponlop, Dzogchen. *Mind Beyond Death.* Boston, MA: Shambhala Publications, 2008.

Rigpa Shedra Wiki, an Online Encyclopedia. "Tukdam," n.d. https://www.rigpawiki.org/index.php?title=Tukdam.

Rigpa Shedra Wiki, an Online Encyclopedia. "Vajra Body," n.d. https://www.rigpawiki.org/index.php?title=Vajra_body.

Rinchen, Geshe Sonam. *Atisha's Lamp for the Path to Enlightenment.* Translated by Ruth Sonam. First Edition. Ithaca, NY: Snow Lion, 1997.

Rinpoche., Dzogchen Ponlop. "Song from the Heart: Commentary by Dzogchen Ponlop on Kagyu Mahamudra Supplication." *Bodhi Magazine* 8, no. 2 (2007): 3.

Rinpoche, Yongey Mingyur, and Eric Swanson. *The Joy of Living: Unlocking the Secret and Science of Happiness.* New York, NY: Harmony/Rodale, 2008.

Rinpoche's New Book Available For Download. "Khyentse Foundation." Accessed September 23, 2023. https://khyentsefoundation.org/preview-of-rinpoches-new-book-available-for-download/.

Solomo, Erric. "Interview with Adeu Rinpoche for Chokling Tersar Times." Erik Pema Kunsang Among Masters: A Live Biography, October 3, 1999. http://erik-pema-kunsang-a-live-biography.blogspot.com/p/blog-page_3367.html.

Trungpa, Chogyam. *Cutting Through Spiritual Materialism.* Boston, MA: Shambhala Publications, 2002.

———. *Meditation in Action.* Berkeley, CA: Shambala Publications, 1970.

———. *Ocean of Dharma: The Everyday Wisdom of Chogyam Trungpa.* Shambhala Publications, 2008.

———. *Shambhala: The Sacred Path of the Warrior.* Berkeley, CA: Shambhala Publications, 1984.

———. *The Bodhisattva Path of Wisdom and Compassion: The Profound Treasury of the Ocean of Dharma, Volume Two*. Edited by Judith L. Lief. Boston, MA: Shambhala Publications, 2013.

———. *The Collected Works of Chogyam Trungpa*. Edited by Carolyn Rose Gimian. Vol. 8. Boston, MA: Shambhala Publications, 2004.

———. *The Collected Works of Chögyam Trungpa: The Art of Calligraphy*. Vol. 7. The Collected Works of Chögyam Trungpa. Boston, MA: Shambhala Publications, 2010.

Trungpa, Chögyam. *The Essential Chogyam Trungpa*. Edited by Carolyn Rose Gimian. Boston, MA: Shambhala Publications, 1999.

———. *The Heart Of The Buddha*. Shambhala Publications, 1991.

———. *The Myth of Freedom and the Way of Meditation*. Boulder, CO: Shambhala Publications, 1976.

———. *The Path of Individual Liberation: The Profound Treasury of the Ocean of Dharma, Volume One*. Edited by Judith L. Lief. Shambhala Publications, 2013.

———. *The Tantric Path of Indestructible Wakefulness*. Edited by Judith L. Lief. Illustrated edition. Vol. 3. The Profound Treasury of the Ocean of Dharma. Boston, MA: Shambhala, 2013.

Tsoknyi Rinpoche. "Rinpoche Discusses Retreat." Pundarika Foundation, June 26, 2017. https://tsoknyirinpoche.org/yeshe-rangsal/places-to-practice-2/an-interview-concerning-retreat-with-tsoknyi-rinpoche/.

Zangmo, Sherab. Interview by James Gritz, 2005.

www.ingramcontent.com/pod-product-compliance
Lightning Source LLC
Chambersburg PA
CBHW050928240426
43671CB00019B/2958